Advance Praise for

I Wish I'd Known That Earlier in My Career: The Power of Positive Workplace Politics

Horan's book of real-life examples weaves cross-cultural and gender insights to accurately reframe a perennial subject—power and politics. Her book shows why both understanding and gaining the right skills to deal with the politics inherent in any organization is critical for an individual's success. For those interested in political savvy as a fundamental leadership skill, this is a great read for anyone within a large or small organization operating across cultures and communities.

Steve Milovich
Senior Vice President, Global Human Resources & Talent Diversity
Disney ABC Television

Politics in organizations surrounds us but defining and and analyzing it is both personal and challenging. Most of us have ambivalent feelings towards organizational politics and unsure whether to own up to its existence. Jane Horan addresses the dilemma in dealing with organizational politics extremely effectively, putting the process in the right perspective and showing how to maneuver between good and not-so-good politics. *I Wish I'd Known That Earlier in My Career* provides clear roadmaps to help the readers reframe their thinking, giving real-life examples and interactive guidelines on how to strategically engage the organization. Highly recommended!

Girish Vaidya
Former Senior Vice President and Head of Infosys Leadership Institute
Founder Director, IncValue Advisors Pvt Ltd.

Feel like a cultural misfit in today's gringo-global corporate political discourse? If ya' can't beat 'em, join 'em. Horan's book is your guide. It provides a mindset to wear and actions to take to "hitch up" to the system if you hope to make it or make a difference.

Dr. George Simons
Founder of Diversophy
Author of *EuroDiversity: A Business Guide to Managing Difference*

Political forces in your organization are inevitable: the point is, to make political skills a constructive part of your leadership toolkit [framework] to enhance your contribution. In *I Wish I'd Known That Earlier In My Career*, Horan provides a valuable reference to understand and navigate culture, gender and the power of positive politics—insightful and actionable.

Andrew Hanna
Former Managing Director, Sparrowhawk Media, Asia Pacific
Managing Director, Clearview Data, Australia

An excellent guide for negotiating the challenges of the corporate world.

Dr Gareth Morgan
Distinguished Research Professor
Schulich School of Business, York University
Author, *Images of Organization*

I Wish I'd Known That Earlier In My Career

Funded by
MISSION COLLEGE
Carl D. Perkins Vocational and Technical Education Act Grant

I Wish I'd Known That Earlier In My Career

The Power of Positive Workplace Politics

Jane Horan

WILEY

John Wiley & Sons (Asia) Pte. Ltd

Published in 2012 by John Wiley & Sons (Asia) Pte. Ltd.
1 Fusionopolis Walk, #07–01, Solaris South Tower, Singapore 138628

This publication is designed to provide accurate and authoritative information in regard to the
subject matter covered. It is sold with the understanding that the publisher is not engaged in
rendering professional services. If professional advice or other expert assistance is required,
the services of a competent professional person should be sought.

Neither the authors nor the publisher are liable for any actions prompted or caused by the
information presented in this book. Any views expressed herein are those of the authors and do
not represent the views of the organizations they work for.

Other Wiley Editorial Offices
John Wiley & Sons, 111 River Street, Hoboken, NJ 07030, USA
John Wiley & Sons, The Atrium, Southern Gate, Chichester, West Sussex, P019 8SQ, United
    Kingdom
John Wiley & Sons (Canada) Ltd., 5353 Dundas Street West, Suite 400, Toronto, Ontario,
    M9B 6HB, Canada
John Wiley & Sons Australia Ltd., 42 McDougall Street, Milton, Queensland 4064, Australia
Wiley-VCH, Boschstrasse 12, D-69469 Weinheim, Germany

Library of Congress Cataloging-in-Publication Data

ISBN: 978-0470-82968-4 (Paperback)
ISBN: 978-0470-82970-7 (ePDF)
ISBN: 978-0470-82969-1 (Mobi)
ISBN: 978-0470-82971-4 (ePub)

Typeset in 12/16pts Times Roman by MPS Limited, a Macmillan Company

Printed in Singapore by Markono Print Media Pte. Ltd

10   9   8   7   6   5   4   3   2

To my mother,
1927–1978

Contents

Acknowledgments

If it takes a village to raise a child, the same holds for writing a book—especially one with global applications. This book would have never made it to print had there not been so many people I have had the good fortune to know and learn from along the way.

Watching good (and not-so-good) managers rise to the top, I always wondered "Why?" Hearing the whispers of "politics, politics, politics," I thought I knew why. A day with Marty Seldman brought everything together for me, although a global financial crisis and redundancy after six months in a new country gave clarity I was not expecting. As the old Yiddish saying goes "Man plans and God laughs."

Marty Seldman and John Futterknecht are two inspirational executive coaches who started me on my continuous journey of learning about politics and power inside organizations. I am humbled by their wisdom, phenomenal support and guidance along this learning path. But I wouldn't have met Marty had it not been for Steve Milovich, a savvy HR leader with a generous soul. And I would not have met Steve had it not been for Philippe Gas, an intelligent, insightful and humble leader with a genuine gift in helping others achieve greatness. I have learned many insights from Disney executives, particularly Andy Bird, Brian Spaulding, Jeff Paule, Keith Busch, Henrietta Summers, Bill Frew, Jim Lygopolous, Karin Blumquist, Sharon Saxton, David Yudis, Sadie Stern, Glenn Rosen, Barbara Howes, Jim Howard, Drew Hayashida, Joe Rohde, Laurent Riffault, Vivian Chong, Jessica Kam, Randy Chee, Marilyn Ardito, Laura Wendt, Mai Tatoy, Emily Wong, Elsa Ng, Jean Marie Cacciatore, Nicky Douglas, Rich Ross, and many, many others. My time at Kraft, too, provided valuable insights and for these I am grateful and indebted to James Andrade, Varun Bhatia, and Jin Montesano.

I am deeply thankful to Simon Baddeley and Kim James for their patient correspondence, guidance and incredible knowledge in political behavior, from which I learned something new each time. Along that virtual path, I have corresponded with Sam Culbert and appreciate his wit and wisdom on performance-management systems. My writing and thinking about positive politics has been influenced by many scholars in this area: Jeffrey Pfeffer, David Buchanan, Tanya Arroba, Gareth Morgan, Lee Bohman, Terrence Deal, Robert Sutton, Art Kleiner, Andrew DuBrin, Annette Simmons, and Robert Greene.

The seeds of this book were planted at a workshop I gave on the Power of Positive Politics at the Women's International Network Conference in Prague in 2009, when participants asked, "Has anyone written a book on this?" They were watered the following day when Jo Parfaitt offered coaching sessions for would-be authors, and they have grown and taken shape in the form of the book in your hands. Along the way, I have met and had support from many powerful women, including Vered Neta, and Fran O'Hara.

As I began conducting my savvy workshops in Asia, Stavros Yiannouka shared his ideas on the definition of positive politics and I am grateful to him for this. Two women in particular, Sung Hae

Kim and Rie Rumito—fellow mothers, HR gurus, smart, savvy and very grounded—both offered help when I needed it most, and this book has many of their professional insights and comments woven through. I owe both of them, and words cannot express my gratitude.

Everyone has a story and my stories come from many places—the soccer pitch and the supermarket checkout, as well as from my workshops and from listening to presentations from colleagues in faraway places. I would like to thank Laurie Clark, Cathy Bayless, Diane Brady, Donna Martin, Christy Davis, Lucy Lei, Khatiza Van Savage, Susan Gas, Anna Lee, Leslie Taylor, Irene Tsang, Lesley Lewis, Kate Michelson Tracy Ann Curtis, Ruth Shapiro, Fiona Connell, Libby Armstrong, Cairine Haslam, Gokul Chandar, Janice Armstrong, Marlene Han, Nancy Pahor, Janine Stein, Linda Laddin, Alexandra Von Ilsemann, Priscilla Chan, Kathy Geller, Jessica Khine, Alison Harbert, David Haskell, Hayden Majajas, Matt Chapman, Julie Ann Ashton, Mathilda VanWyk, Teresa Devashayam, Astrid Tuminez, Anne Lochoff, Jill Herriott, Emma Boyd, J. Feb. Horan, P. Bakers, John C. Horan and the late Helen Maguire Horan and Pegs Morris.

Many wonderful stories and insights have come from questions at my workshops. I would like to acknowledge the following professional networks: PrimeTime, Thinking Women's Group, Women's Media Network, The Women's Foundation of Hong Kong, Financial Women's Association, WIN, The American Chamber of Commerce in Hong Kong and Singapore, SIM, SMU, NUS, and women's networks at British Telecom, GE, Nomura, UBS, NSN, Société Générale, Hewlett Packard, McGraw Hill, Medtronics, Colgate Palmolive, Covidien, P&G, Shell, McDonald's and Microsoft. To the countless unnamed women I have coached in savvy, I am forever grateful for your insights, your knowledge, and your willingness to share as openly as you have.

Many serendipitous events have happened in the course of writing and publishing this book. After I gave a presentation at The

American Chamber of Commerce in Singapore, I met CJ Hwu, Wiley's Publishing Editor. Prior to this meeting, I'd sent a proposal to John Wilig, and am thankful to both CJ and John for taking a risk with a first-time writer. I soon met the wonderful Wiley team: Nick Melchior, Janis Soo, Karin Seet, and my fantastic editor, John Owen, who has the editor's knack for reshaping and rewriting, and doing so with grace and wit—not an easy thing. I have learned much from this group of professionals and sincerely appreciate their guidance and unyielding support.

Saving the most important for last—when I first met Neal Horwitz I knew he was my soulmate. This book would not have ever been written without his encouragement, guidance, support, insights, and love. He is a true savvy coach, always asking the right questions, forcing me to think differently on any topic. We have two beautiful children, Hank and Elah Horwitz, and I am grateful for their patience and forbearance as I disappeared into my office many, many times to write just one more story. They have been involved with this labor of love from the beginning, and I thank them for it.

Foreword

In June 1986, I started my career as an executive coach. At that time coaching was not looked on as an integral part of leadership development, as it is now. In fact, many of the executives who were assigned to coaching were resistant. They were mostly aggressive, competitive individuals, not very self-aware, and I used to routinely hear comments like "I don't want to go to a shrink" or "The company is sending me to charm school." Then, in the mid-90s, I noticed a distinct shift in the kind of people who came to my program. They were smart, competent, with great values, a good work ethic and getting decent results. What they also had in common was that their careers were stalling as a result of major blind spots they had about organizational politics.

As I dug deeper into each situation, I would see people who were routinely underestimated, "pigeon-holed," bad-mouthed and marginalized, who were not getting full credit for their work and being unfairly blamed when things didn't go well. They lacked the awareness and skills they needed to deal with people who didn't operate with the same principles they did.

So this is what prompted me, with my wife Kelly Reineke, who was doing research on power differences and communication, to develop an Organizational Savvy model. The goal was to help these deserving individuals acquire the skills they needed to reach their full career potential.

When the corporate scandals exploded in 2000, just from reading the business page every day it became apparent the kind of damage that an overly political person could do to a company's resources and reputation. If someone like this, without a moral compass and who puts their own interests over the company's, got into a position of power, it was only a matter of time before they hurt the company.

This was when Rick Brandon and I decided to offer Organizational Savvy seminars. Our goal was to reach larger numbers of individuals in a company and to provide an additional focus. We wanted to teach leaders how to identify and deal with overly political people. The added components included how to detect deception and how to know who to trust and who not to trust. As the seminar spread to many companies, including Disney, I had the good fortune to meet and collaborate with Jane Horan. I am thrilled that she has devoted herself, her coaching and consulting practice to expanding our understanding of organizational politics. In particular, Jane has given us a clear line of sight into gender and cultural applications of savvy. Her work with female executives and years of living in Asia are reflected in the many case studies and career tips that enrich the book.

I believe her work will help many individuals continue to advance their careers in an ethical, savvy way, and help companies identify and elevate leaders with the right values.

Marty Seldman, PhD
Co-author, *Survival of the Savvy*

Introduction
Why We Don't Move Ahead—*Politics*

Sitting in the kitchen at the age of 13, listening and watching my mother talk to my grandmother (the most politically shrewd woman on the planet) about challenges at work, I was always puzzled. I couldn't figure out what was happening, as she recounted her day after working eight hours at the hospital, watching the pained look on her face as she would stand over the sink washing vegetables while preparing dinner. The stories seemed trite to me, and yet were tinged with trouble as she spoke.

She would often start with something such as, "The charge nurse said this to the surgeon and the surgeon said this to the nurse," and the dialogue had absolutely nothing to do with medicine. Sometimes it was about real work issues, but mostly about who did what to whom.

With integrity as her backbone and equity her driving force, my mother, then Director of Nurses and Surgical Head Nurse of a large hospital, reported to a medical committee and later testified in court about a botched surgery of a famous surgeon in which someone died. After fretting for days on whether or not to testify, she did what was right from an ethical point of view. Soon after, she was reassigned to an administrative position (at the same hospital), something she neither liked nor was passionate about—all because she spoke the truth to power and suffered the consequences.

This decision took its toll on her in more ways than one. Maintaining a professional outlook while harboring resentment about what went on inside hospitals, she passed away early in life from cancer. Forty years later, I've observed, witnessed and listened to similar stories within multinationals. Things haven't changed much in the past four decades; unfortunately, many women still overlook the political aspects of the workplace.

My father dealt with politics by "hitching his wagon to someone powerful" early in his career. He started with General Motors on an assembly line, but was soon bored with the monotony of lining auto parts in a box and tired of the maneuverings of factory workers. He wasn't politically astute, but had an intrinsic understanding of power. A powerful young manager noticed him, tapped him on the shoulder with advice and support to move into management. He listened and never looked back. He worked for this boss for over 30 years, never said a bad word about him and moved along at his side—even in retirement my father moved to the same city his boss had settled in.

Since those early years in the kitchen, I've been a keen observer of people, watching the moves, set-ups, sabotage and, I should add, many acts of kindness. Starting in sales, I made my way to Human Resources, thinking my intuitive sense would be an asset to organizations and a good fit for me. In HR, I learned much about human behavior, and even more about politics inside organizations. Reflecting back on my mother's stories, I now fully understand her angst.

When I worked for the Walt Disney Company, I was fortunate to have met Dr Marty Seldman, an authentic, insightful and intuitive professional. Marty co-authored (with Rick Brandon) the book *Survival of the Savvy*, which opened my eyes and was the impetus to study more on power and politics within organizations. Marty's course, "Organizational Savvy," turned out to be one of the more popular courses at Disney. I clearly remember reading through the syllabus and finding the write-up distasteful. I couldn't believe the company was offering a course to smooth the ruffled feathers of managers who had never "made it." Sitting for years behind the desk, working ungodly hours, these were the perfectionists that were often overlooked for promotions, yet always at the company's beck and call to do more when asked.

The course had received such interest that management wanted to run the program in Asia. I was reluctant to roll out anything that smacked of "politics," and when I went back to Disney headquarters in Burbank California the following month, I made a side trip to Berkeley to meet Marty and ask about the course. From that eight-hour, one-on-one session, everything came together for me. I started to look differently not only at organizations but at life. At last, my mother's story (and those of many other women executives) made perfect sense.

I soon started teaching organizational savvy at work and using these skills to coach executives. I saw that many people either shied away from politics or simply denied the existence of politics. Naive and innocent, they worked long hours, followed the rules, and were consummate at every detail. Listening to the voices of these people in casual conversation, I would hear what I took to be innocuous comments. At first I thought little of it, but soon heard the patterns of career-limiting remarks:

- "I don't need to toot my own horn; my work speaks for itself."
- "I've got a full-time job and family; I don't have time to play these asinine games."
- "Networking? Do you have any idea how much I've got on my plate? I have no time—or interest—to go to lunch, or any of these power breakfasts."
- "I have deadlines. I don't have time for this petty stuff, and nor do I want to be viewed as a brown-noser."

For anyone, male or female, being able to navigate the political waters inside organizations is a critical leadership skill and a building block for success. Politics—in the true sense of the word—is about building coalitions and managing company affairs. As Seldman highlights in *Survival of the Savvy,* politics is often negatively defined; yet political astuteness, combined with the right values, will always have a positive outcome for the individual and organization. A lack of political awareness is not only detrimental: the mere mention of this word raises eyebrows, causes elbows to cross, and elicits the common rejoinder, "We have no politics here."

How do we change perceptions and learn to accept what is, in order to fully engage and embrace the complete organization? One force driving this change is women—or, rather, the lack of women—getting to the top. While there are plenty of books about workplace bullying, little has been written on the subtle side of organizational life—politics and power: who has it and how to obtain it.

The politically savvy understand and have access to power, know how to get ideas sold and move up the organization more quickly than others. While politics is not viewed positively and rarely discussed (except in negative terms), it's always present inside organizations, regardless of size. Multinationals, NGOs and academic institutions are all rife with politics. I recently sent an email to a consultant working for the UN, as I had heard they were looking for diversity experts. I mentioned on my note that I taught a course on *positive* politics. "So you want to teach politics to the most political organization in the world?" came her incredulous reply.

I had originally titled my workshops "Organizational Savvy," but quickly changed and renamed the course for what it is: "Politics"—a critical yet elusive leadership skill.

Many of us don't talk about politics and, if we do, it's at the water cooler or at a coffee shop or watering hole with our close friends. Politics is rarely taught in organizations or business schools. Yet it's always present. But what is political savvy? Politics is about power and power bases. We all need to acknowledge and be aware of the unwritten rules of operating inside organizations, accepting and embracing the political side of organizational life, and having the skills and intuition to navigate successfully.

Savvy is having the skill to navigate politics. Politics—or being political—can be negative or positive.

- The positive definition of organizational politics: Building coalitions for the good of the organization.
- The negative side of politics: Building coalitions for the good of the self only.

In his book *Images of Organizations,* Gareth Morgan, a distinguished research professor in Organizational Behavior at York University in Canada, had this to say:

> One of the curious features of organizational life is that although many people know they are surrounded by organizational politics they rarely come out and say so. One ponders politics in private moments or discusses it off the record with close confidants and friends or in the context of one's own political maneuverings with members of one's coalition.[1]

A savvy manager *knows the unwritten rules at work but rarely talks about them.* And many of us put our heads down and work harder, believing that this will keep us away from the game of politics. But *if we don't learn these skills, we'll never get ahead* (and, worse yet, organizations will lose very talented people who drop out of this never-ending "rat-race").

Many professionals cite politics as the main reason they leave organizations and start their own businesses. It's critical for all of us in business to understand and embrace the political side of organizational life for career and business success, employing political behavior that is grounded in ethics, values and for the good of the organization.

Whenever I deliver these "political" workshops, I often get the same reactions. Some cry, seeing themselves in the case studies, or realizing they've been caught up in the nasty side of politics. Others decide they still don't want to engage in the political side of the organization. And the rest are completely thrilled with their new set of skills. The courses are part common sense, part intuition, and all about the willingness to participate in the whole organization— which is to confidently enter into the political arena. Interestingly enough, the ones I've viewed as most savvy *always* ask for a private coaching session with me.

This book is about politics, but not the bullying or intimidating part. Rather, it is the subtle side—the side you know, feel and sense but can't always articulate. This book brings the elephant fully into the room, sharing stories about the politically aware and unaware. It is written for all ages, levels, professions, and cultures to enable everyone to engage in the complete organization and to operate with ethics and values while being politically astute.

ENDNOTE

1. Morgan (1997).

CHAPTER 1

The How and Why
of Positive Politics

What do the politically savvy know and what is it exactly that they do? Mention the word "politics" in any setting and everyone cringes. Yet there are two sides to being politically savvy: the negative—the overly political operator, preoccupied with self; and the positive—the overly political leader, focused on the organization or group. Walk the hallways at work and hear the choir sing "He/She is so political" and take note. We all think we know what this means, but do we? It is used frequently, but almost never with a defined meaning. Others believe politics is analogous to pornography; you know it when you see it! The truth of the matter is you can be overly political and be out for the good of the group, yet most of us view politicians as being out only for themselves.

Who comes to mind when you think "politics"? Hillary Clinton, George Bush, Angela Merkel, Hu Jin Tao, Barack Obama? If we examine presidential politics, we hear and see the ugly side of politics. Certainly everyone has an opinion about these leaders, yet how interesting that Merkel and Clinton are belittled for what they wear, how they look or speak. They're labeled for outward appearances; matronly, frumpy or fat. Sarah Palin is interesting for the opposite reason, looking more attractive than not, appealing to a non-traditional demographic group, and able to gather national attention as an "underdog" politician.

For men, the same applies. As one wag said many years ago, "The US will never elect a bald president." While men do not have to watch their looks as much as women do, it would be silly to think that looks, dress, and deportment do not play a large role for them too. It's easy to see how politics weaves in and out of the boardrooms, and is often divisive and negative. Yet people still enter into public service, and many more want to lead organizations.

If we profile successful CEOs, aren't they all political? Yes. Political savvy is a critical leadership skill—not one learned at a business school course but, rather, through trial, error, failures and mistakes. Some men learn this intuitively. Unfortunately, many women don't. Yet, ironically, it is the women who are often more intuitive. Understanding and accepting politics is the first step in knowing what is needed to be part of the organization.

DEFINING POLITICS

Politics is a fact of organizational life and needs to be put into proper perspective. Yet creating a clear and succinct definition of politics is not easy. Politics fundamentally is about power, power bases, power sources, power shifts and power dynamics. Henry Mintzberg, a professor of Management at McGill University, looks at politics as "Individual or group behavior that is informal, typically divisive, and in a technical sense, illegitimate, not sanctioned by formal authority, nor certified expertise."[1]

Brandon and Seldman (2004) have taken a slightly different view, seeing politics as the art or science of "informal, unofficial, and sometimes behind-the-scenes efforts to sell ideas, influence an organization, increase power or achieve other targeted objectives." This definition is spot on.

UNOFFICIAL AND BEHIND THE SCENES

Heading back to the US to attend a meeting at Disney in Burbank, I learned a valuable lesson in political savvy: the impact of behind-the-scenes lobbying. Disney executives used to travel frequently from Tokyo to Burbank, so much so that the United Airlines Tokyo–Los Angeles flight resembled a Disney boardroom. The mid-afternoon flight buzzed with laptops, video presentations, pointer pens and laughter.

Just before the plane took off, a well-groomed gentleman wearing the requisite khaki pants and light-blue oxford button-down shirt, asked if I would mind changing seats with him so that he could spend the long flight strategizing with his boss for their meetings in Burbank. I obliged.

I was then seated next to a man with a full beard, a long ponytail cascading down his back and silver amulets hanging off the lobe of his left ear. He was not a typical "suit." At his sandaled feet was a stack of coffee-table books, enough to stock a small book shop. Sizing him up, I thought he was either a professor or an anthropologist: he couldn't possibly be a businessman.

First impressions can be wrong. He introduced himself: I was sitting next to a senior executive with an entertainment company, Frank. He had been working in Bhutan when he received a personal summons from his boss, the CEO, to return to discuss budgets and projects.

On that 12-hour plane ride, I learned more about executive teams and how decisions are made than I ever learned in graduate school. An ordinary flight turned into a college course on the role of power networks and how organizations work.

I couldn't imagine what that meeting with this CEO would be like. Highly creative, he was said to have the attention span of a gnat and little patience for any pauses in presentations. With executives like this, you need to be a good stump speaker. I have watched many fall from grace over poor presentations or being ill prepared.

Frank seemed unconcerned, though, seeing the meeting as a formality since his boss already knew "all the pieces." That being the case, I ventured, why bother going back for a formality?

During the course of the conversation, however, it became clear that for Frank, formality was, as he put it, "a serious agenda—if you don't care, then why should the others?" Frank had been doing this for more than 20 years.

Although the preparation and conversation may take place ahead of time, the meeting is (to use Frank's words) "a ceremony in the most ancient and venerable sense." To Frank and other executives, "being present symbolizes commitment and commitment builds trust."

Frank told me how he had been on the phone with the CEO and others to lay out plans for projects. During the calls, he had felt resistance and challenges on deadlines and budgets. Frank was affable and bright, and had a good relationship with his boss and the project team. He ensured that all parties concerned understood the project clearly and framed their arguments, for or against, around the same values. The CEO knew the project in detail and agreed with the strategy. "By the time we get to the meetings, everyone's on board. I'm flying back to show my face." As Frank indicated, and I certainly came to know, this was "culture-building and a signature of commitment." For Frank and other executives, these decisions are complex, interconnected and have a long-term impact on the company.

There's an important lesson here: while slick presentation is important, time spent before the presentation is invaluable for building momentum, understanding, and acceptance that is needed long before the meeting starts. While many managers think this is manipulation or gamesmanship—it's not.

Rarely is one meeting enough to discuss all the elements of a complex project, business strategy, or acquisition properly. Discussing ideas before the formal meeting has multiple benefits; from building stakeholders, understanding resistance and, ultimately, resulting in more innovative solutions or ideas.

This pre-meeting discussion allows *thinking time.* Thinking time is a precious commodity that we rarely have time for. The idea then becomes embedded in the collective thought process, enabling collaborative decision making to take place more easily.

Ultimately, as Frank put it, you want everyone at the meeting "to visualize and conceptualize the project naturally and spontaneously, not just as a bullet point on a chart." In his view, "meetings are for going over numbers and details but for a leader to be effective, particularly in meetings, they need a concrete image of the project. This takes time and multiple points of access" such that "by the time you're at the meeting, the image is formed and the decisions are modeled."

Did it help, I asked, being connected to the CEO, or any CEO for that matter?

"I had the ability to call [him] but my access to him was used carefully, not wasted," Frank said. "We had a working relationship based on empathic casualness and openness." It was not about power or status. "My access is predicated on what I have to say," Frank said.

More than anything, he added, "It is important to cultivate a culture of thought around a project, have meaningful contact with decision-makers prior to making decisions. With that, there needs to be space for structured dialogue, dissent that is productive, not destructive, within the group in any organization—whether at my work or anyplace else."

For me, the penny dropped.

Thinking back to Seldman's definition of politics, coalition building and lobbying behind the scenes is necessary, positive and smart. Lobbying behind the scenes influences reluctant team members while promoting and furthering the cause of others, hopefully for the good of the organization. Using political tactics for the good of the organization is not about sabotage or unethical behavior. It makes sense. Organizations are made up of people with different perspectives, agendas and interests. (For Frank, too, it was important to take account of "the humanity of corporate culture . . . the specific person-ness of each person in the chain.")

The important point is to focus on the interests of the consumers and ensure their needs are being met. Some managers find it challenging to balance the cost and time in building coalitions, lobbying support and their day job. It is a skill, and luckily one that can be learned.

Being savvy is about understanding the unwritten rules about how organizations work, to sell ideas and for career growth. Being a savvy and successful lobbyist requires a thorough understanding of the organizational culture. Culture plays a significant role in politics and determines what skills are necessary, and when and how to use them.

WHY IT IS IMPORTANT TO EMBRACE POLITICS

There's a wealth of research and books on corporate politics for the politically challenged, the cynical and the naive. Jeffrey Pfeffer, Professor of Organizational Behavior at Stanford University Graduate School of Business, has researched and written extensively on power inside organizations. Two former professors, Lee Bohman and Terrence Deal, discuss politics and links to deception within organizations.[2] In the UK, Baddeley and James (1990) look at the dynamics of political management and publish books on political skills for managers. Along with Seldman and Brandon, these authors reiterate the importance of embracing the political side of organizations with ethics and integrity, as well as the need to challenge deception and negative political behavior.

When we think about deception, Enron and WorldCom may come to mind, along with the downfall of Wall Street banks at the end of 2008. Bohman and Deal (2008) highlight the demise of Kohlberg, Kravis, Roberts & Co. (KKR), which was in no small way a study in greed and self-serving politics. KKR's managing partners were masters of the leveraged buy-out (LBO), a management practice in vogue in the 1980s. Its LBO of RJR Nabisco is a classic case of misused politics for the good of a few. The US$25-billion deal spurred a book and a movie, *Barbarians at the Gate*. *Time* magazine called it a "Game of Greed" and it is still one of the most read books on buy-outs.[3]

In 2008, Bear Stearns and Lehman Brothers collapsed, leaving a global trail of devastation. While much has been written about the fall of these two giants from a financial perspective—particularly the exposure to mortgage-backed assets in the subprime mortgage crisis—it's also easy to pinpoint politics. *The New York Daily News* (see Fishman 2008) chronicled the relationships and fiefdoms within the investment banking community, highlighting self-serving politics, siloed thinking, and scapegoats. Some believe that Lehman CEO Richard Fuld was sacrificed so others could be saved. When Fuld reached out for help from Hank Paulson, former Chairman and CEO of Goldman Sachs and then US Secretary of the Treasury, his requests fell on deaf ears. As one commentator put it: "Paulson—for reasons Fuld doesn't yet understand—participated in making him a scapegoat" (Chapman 2010). For many involved with the near-collapse of the banks in September 2008, questions still remain as to why Lehman and Bear Stearns fell.

Chapman, Jagger (2010) and others affirm that Lehman's fate was determined by Fuld's rivals, Paulson included: "Fuld and his allies can't help but blame Paulson, whom he'd trusted and, until the end, viewed as an ally and even a friend."[4]

The banks themselves were hardly blameless, suffering from outrageous errors in judgment and egos in overdrive. But Fuld had a paucity of savvy skills. Throughout his tenure at Lehman, he never managed to build bridges and connections with Wall Street's power elite and he has been vilified as Wall Street's "Gorilla" and other pejorative remarks (Chapman 2010; Jagger 2010).

Why is it so important to learn savvy skills? Brandon and Seldman (2004) highlight the need for leaders across the organization to recognize and stop deception, destructive politics and selfish agendas. Learning savvy skills heightens the awareness of deception, distortion and agendas when people and organizations start heading down the wrong path. Savvy skills force people to raise their hands and find their voices when organizations go astray. The failure of these organizations impacts the social structure of society. KKR was the largest failed merger in the history of US business. How many employees lost their jobs during the KKR merger? Thousands. Who reaped the benefits? Very few. How many people lost their life savings when Lehman closed? Many.

> Business school students need to learn the principles of power . . . it is possible to teach them the importance of political skill to their success . . .
>
> (Pfeffer 2010)

Enron's Sherron Watkins, VP of Corporate Development, is a good example of uncovering deceit. Watkins repeatedly told her bosses, Kenneth Lay and Jeffrey Skilling, that Enron needed to come clean on the finances, alluding to the potential implosion of the firm in a detailed seven-page memo. The day after she spoke up, the CFO, Andrew Fastow, wanted her fired and her computer seized. Yet she survived and went on to be named *Time* magazine's Person of the Week.[5]

It's time organizations and individuals began to embrace the inevitable and learn how to navigate the fundamentals of organizational life. Political savvy is a critical, elusive leadership skill that business schools and organizations need to embrace and teach. Providing this knowledge builds engagement and maintains talent. Too many talented individuals are passed over for promotions, made redundant or leave organizations because they either don't understand how to work with politics or they refuse to do so. Instead, they put their heads down, remain invisible and work harder. And by doing so, they are the first ones on the chopping block during a redundancy, layoff or merger.

ENDNOTES

1. G. L. Adams, D. C. Treadway and L. P. Stepina 2008. "The role of disposition in politics perception formation: The predictive capacity of

negative and positive affectivity, equity sensitivty, and self-efficacy." *Journal of Managerial Issues*, Winter.
2. See Bohman and Deal (2008).
3. Ross Johnson, RJR Nabisco's CEO, and Henry Kravis of KKR entered a bidding war to take RJR Nabisco private. After millions of dollars were spent between lawyers, bankers and brokers, the result was a few individuals gaining significant sums, taking on a new company and an iconic brand left in tatters.
4. Fishman (2008).
5. January 18, 2002.

CHAPTER 2

Becoming Savvy

Sarah's Story

Sarah was a lawyer in the legal department of a large multinational corporation. She stood out as the poster child for self-promotion: she was incredibly skillful at talking about herself, her credo being "If I don't do it, who will?"

She was a mid-level lawyer in a regional team of seven. Though she was not as experienced as the others, and hadn't graduated from a top law school, people always seemed to listen to her counsel.

Sarah came from a working-class family in South Africa. Her father had bought and sold many businesses, and not always profitably. But, with government assistance, they'd got by. Sarah understood the ups and downs of her life, and considered herself a "survivor." She had put herself through school with no financial assistance, married young, had three children by age 25 and managed to graduate from law school. She believed in hard work without handouts.

(continued)

Sarah was a large-boned woman of medium height, dressed well and had a noticeable stridency to her voice. When she walked into the room, everyone knew it. She had a knack for seeking out the most powerful person in the room within seconds, reaching out with a firm handshake, stating her name, saying what she'd accomplished and what new projects she was working on. She was a natural self-promoter. A powerhouse of activity, Sarah would always take on additional work, saying: "Oh, I'll take care of that" or "Consider it done." Some considered her a bully, with an attitude that was sometimes interpreted as brusque, and she was never slow to present herself in a good light, even at the expense of her colleagues.

In one pivotal meeting, Sarah sat next to the Senior Partner, listening quietly and studying the room. Ruth, a junior lawyer with dual law degrees from Harvard and Oxford, had been invited to present on new client projects. Just before the presentation was due to begin, Sarah spoke to her across the table: "When I was in Madrid last week, our [largest European] client called me asking for guidance on how to get counsel; he said something about no-one returning his calls. 'You're kidding,' I told him. 'That can't be right; we have our best lawyers on your case.'"

With a concerned look, the senior partner interjected: "Ruth, isn't that one of your clients?"

Ruth was speechless. Prior to the meeting, she had been a little nervous and Sarah had been so encouraging, telling her to "just show up and be yourself." Why hadn't she mentioned the call then?

Sarah may not have been the most popular person among her colleagues but she was always prepared. Every time she joined a meeting, she had her pitch ready and would tell people what she did, even if they didn't ask or care. She was a big personality with little humor and never hesitated to let people know how much she knew, even when what she knew may have had no direct relevance to the business. Sarah liked to hold court. Adept at name-dropping and appealing to authority, she was on first-name terms with the CEO and let others know the important people she met or had lunch with. Earlier in her career, she had been asked to attend a course at Harvard Law School, which she translated into an advanced leadership course for legal professionals aspiring to be CEOs. In her mind, she was top talent, next in line as Chief Counsel. She managed perceptions well, both internally and externally. When the firm acquired smaller boutique firms in other countries, Sarah was given a senior role in charge of integrating new lawyers, and travelled globally to ensure processes, systems and development were in place. With such a strong network, she had ensured a seat for herself at the top table.

We've all seen someone like Sarah, and some may cringe when they read this profile. While I am not advocating being like Sarah, there are aspects of her behavior that we would all do well to learn from. She's known inside the organization as the person who "gets things done." She is connected. I glanced through her LinkedIn[1] profile: she has over 500 contacts and the list is impressive.

Some might regard this type of self-promotion as being ruthlessly self-serving. Indeed, there may be some who may feel they have heard enough of such excesses and will be tempted to stop reading at this point. My advice, though, would be not to give up just yet: there's a great deal that we can learn from people like Sarah and from Ruth's unfortunate experience.

SELF-PROMOTION IS A SKILL

What is self-promotion? Can it be done without feeling like you're chest-beating and bragging? The people I coach find this part of organizational savvy the most difficult to grasp. Often they ask: "Aren't you just teaching me to be someone I'm not?"

While most people may hate the idea, self-promotion is a skill that can and must be learned. Self-promotion is critical for exposure and recognition for you and your team. It is a much-needed leadership skill that is easy to learn and attain. Whether as part of a merger or merely doing your day-to-day job, you need to tell people what you do. There are many opportunities for self-promotion that do not entail abandoning your integrity and values.

In my workshops, I come across many who are prepared to rest on the notion that "My work speaks for itself." Such attitudes fall within what have been called "limiting beliefs" (Broome-Hernez, McLaughlin and Trovas 2009) and are barriers that get in the way of your visibility. Hard work is necessary, but productivity without visibility is not, and rarely overshadows self-promotion.

> To the question "What keeps you from self-promotion?" more than 65 percent responded, "Accomplishments should speak for themselves."
>
> Centre for Creative Leadership (CCL) survey

It's not about being a braggart or loudmouth; it is about reframing your thinking, understanding that your knowledge and what you do is vital to the business. Ask yourself:

- What do I know that can be shared?
- What will help others and also help the organization?

Organizations today are flatter than ever. The recent financial crisis took out another layer of managers and many today are doing three jobs, leaving little time for self-promotion or networking. Right?

Wrong. You need to build self-promotion and networking into your daily routine, as you would with a physical exercise program. Ask yourself what you are doing that your boss or colleagues need to know. The answer will be: plenty.

Your boss probably has more people reporting to him or her than before; it's important, therefore, to keep him/her up to date on what you're doing. The more you state (politely) what you're doing, the better; and keep a record for yourself. Obviously, you need to know how to communicate with your boss. Besides knowing his or her hot buttons or what drives them to distraction, consider mapping your boss from a political perspective, looking at what might be called their Political Quotient (PQ).[2] Is your boss overly political or insufficiently so? Is your boss out for him/herself or for the team and the good of the organization? It is important to know these things before embarking on your self-promotion campaign.

TIPS FOR SELF-PROMOTION

You first must understand the value of self-promotion for you and your team and be able to read the specific situation in which you find yourself and the culture within the company more broadly. Perhaps it is the phrase "self-promotion" itself that is the stumbling block when talking about accomplishments. Yet if you manage a team, or want to move ahead, you must learn how to tell your story—with confidence, not braggadocio. Story-telling with substance is more palatable than self-promotion. Remember, it's not only about you: your story includes your team, those who helped you get to where you are today. The following questions provide steps on how to build your story.

• What are you known for? Build your expert status, internally and externally; become known for something; become the go-to person, the one who knows.
• What have you achieved? Review "to-do" lists, write out activities, business challenges, meetings, and special events that you want to promote. And while you're doing this, create a "not-to-do" list for all activities that keep you away from promoting your team and yourself.
• Who do you know? Create a map of power-brokers and influencers.
• How connected are you? Using your map, send an email to let this group know what you and your team are working on. Don't

just say, "We launched a new marketing plan" or "We created a new engagement survey": tell this group how your project, plan, product or service benefits the business and highlight how this benefits them.

You need to know the *what* and the *how* of self-promotion. The above points are easy to put in place—even if you don't like the sound of self-promotion, these ideas are important for the organization and, more importantly, for your team. If you manage a team, they depend on you to promote and guide them. This is a big hurdle for many to get over, but once you've crossed the line and jumped to the other side it gets easier. This needs to be done on a regular basis when you have something to say and substance to support it. The bottom line is to put your footprint on the organization and a handprint on your work, and then start spreading the news.

Besides self-promotion, you also need to be prepared for chance meetings with those in power and in business meetings. In our example, Ruth was caught off guard by Sarah's comments. Perhaps she had taken too literally Sarah's advice to "just turn up and be yourself." While she may not have been able to anticipate exactly what was to happen, she was perhaps a little naive in being unprepared for the unexpected. While she may well learn from the experience, the damage may have been done already. Wear the hat of a management consultant. Every good consultant goes into every meeting prepared, either with a list of questions or knowing where or how to guide the conversation. Be suspicious of the words, "Just show up; it's casual"—that is seldom the case, as the following story I heard recently demonstrates.

Thomas had been through a series of interviews to become the global head of talent development in a Hong Kong-based company. He'd been informed off the record by the SVP of HR that everyone believed he was the best candidate for the role, implying that an offer of employment would soon be forthcoming. The next day the SVP called to invite him for a "casual" meeting with her boss, Tina. Believing that the meeting was to be a casual meet-and-greet, with no bearing on any forthcoming offer, Thomas showed up casually dressed and not expecting an interview. Tina thanked him for making time on a weekend and reassured him that she had no influence on any decision over the role for which he'd applied. As things turned out, Thomas told me, the meeting didn't go well, as there was little chemistry between the two of them. He was not fazed, however, because he had such great rapport with the others on the team he'd met earlier, all of whom wanted him on board. The following day, he'd received a text from the search firm saying, "You're off the list," with no explanation as to what had happened. Unbeknownst to Thomas, the meeting was not the casual meet-and-greet he had been led to expect. This executive had plenty of power and influence—enough to rescind the offer of employment.

The message here is, never treat any meeting as casual, regardless of what others may call it. Like the Boy Scouts, you need to be prepared at all times.

A POLITICAL MODEL

Researchers Simon Baddeley, Kim Turnbull James and Tanya Arroba have conducted extensive research in organizational politics in the UK over many years. Their work, commissioned by local-government entities, was designed to build middle-management capabilities in political awareness, or what I refer to as "savvy." Their research has been to approach the politics of organizational life with the intention of increasing discussion of such matters in management education programs. In their practice, they teach political sensitivity to managers and field officers across industries and with local-government entities. In order to teach these skills more effectively, they developed a visual model (shown in Figure 2.1 below) using animals to depict the various levels of political awareness and behavior within individuals and organizations.[3]

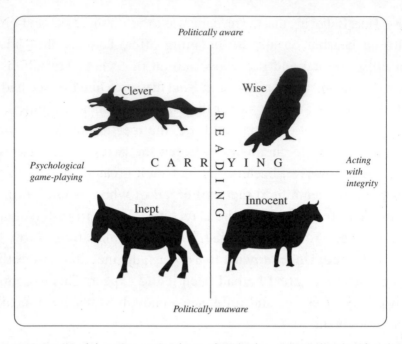

Figure 2.1 Model using animals to depict the various levels of political awareness and behavior within individuals and organizations
Source: Adapted from Baddeley and James (1987)

The model examines four behaviors—wise, clever, inept, and innocent. It is important to emphasize that these behaviors are not cast in stone and can be exhibited in varying degrees by the same person in different situations. As the authors reminded me: "The model is a dynamic behavioral model and not about personality—it's not about taking a quiz to figure out your type. In the course of the day or week you can move across the four quadrants."[4]

In this construction, the Fox is the inner-focused, self-directed, politically aware animal, with a keen understanding of organizational power and influence networks. This behavior may be seen by some as narcissistic.

The astute Owl acts with integrity on behalf of the organization. Like the Fox, the Owl recognizes power and influence and understands who can get things done.

The Donkey operates in a similar fashion to the Fox, but is not as politically shrewd. It sees situations in black and white, and tries hard to be nice but never seems to make it work.

The Sheep, on the other hand, shares the Owl's high values but, like the Donkey, is not politically astute. It acts with integrity, is principled and ethical, but does not recognize power.

As the authors indicate, the animals in the model are really secondary; the real understanding comes from what individuals read and carry into any given situation. They have created a holistic, dynamic model of behavior, a snapshot to frame the landscape within organizations at any given time. This is a necessary step in order to promote ideas. I've met many brilliant managers with brilliant ideas, but who are unable to get traction inside their firm. I've met others who don't understand the "soft dynamics" at work, try to bulldoze their ideas through, fall flat, and fail. In each of these scenarios, both the organization and the individual lose. Many managers know the importance of examining the organization functionally, beyond the day-to-day level, but few are taught the subtleties of political behavior at work.

These authors assert the need to bring this political argot to the surface and make it more transparent and accessible. When using the model in workshops, it is important to reframe thinking around politics—as everyone comes with their own definition and it's usually negative. Politics, both positive and negative, weaves through everyone's workday. At the beginning of one workshop, I asked participants to draw what politics looks like. Their drawings ranged from a sports field, a chess game, and a globe, to a myriad of lines, dots and connections linking people. Almost without exception, the drawings were positive and set the workshop off in a direction that helped shift mindsets. This creative act can get beneath the surface, looking at values, paradoxes and the complicated mix of stakeholders and networks. Reframing the definition provides the participants with a feeling for and an understanding of the positive side of the political arena. Understanding how organizations work by using this model "provides a bridge between the more accessible and rational

aspects of organizational life and the hidden aspects of organizational dynamics" (Baddeley and James 1987). This knowledge might
be considered to be for the privileged few, the domain of exclusive
management-development programs perhaps. However, I hope that
through the pages of this book you too will have access to the same
information to help you maneuver successfully through the organizational maze. As we have seen from the examples of Thomas, Sarah
and Ruth, it is also important to know who calls the shots, who makes
decisions and who has influence. Goleman (1999) regards political
savvy as "reading social and political currents." My argument is that
few people join organizations with these skills intact and few organizations provide opportunities for developing them.

Using this model helps when thinking of your own self-
promotion strategy. Remember Sarah or, in the example in Chapter 1,
recall what Frank and his CEO brought to the meeting, and how to
respond, present or observe.

In their article, James and Arroba (2005) view the model in two
dimensions: Reading and Carrying. Reading refers to the ability to
perceive the less-conspicuous and below-the-surface happenings
inside the organization and is dependent on the frame of reference
(political or non-political) and prior experience that the individual
brings to the situation. Carrying refers to what is carried by the leadership or influence networks in the situation. As the authors explain:

> The dimension of Carrying, managing what is being carried into a
> situation, means having the ability to tune into the internal world
> and be aware of what thoughts and feelings are present, under-
> standing the basis for what is being carried, using this information
> and making conscious choices about action.
>
> On the one hand there was a robust, grounded and integrated
> sense of self being carried into a complex situation: a strong and
> present sense of self enables managers to act calmly, paying attention
> to the task rather than being driven off course by their feelings.
>
> At the other end of the dimension we found evidence of an
> ego-defensive approach being carried: the person felt the need

to protect their feelings rather than focus on the organizational task. Our research found that the more frequently a person was able to manage what they carried and move away from defensive and game-playing behavior and engage a robust, integrated sense of self, the more likely they could behave effectively in situations involving multiple agendas. To be able to 'Read' and 'Carry' well requires managers to become aware of aspects of the organization that are usually not attended to, and even actively avoided because they are perceived to have a negative affect for the organization.

Reading and Carrying are dynamic skills. No context remains static and therefore the ability to Read the context needs to be a dynamic process. For example, taking up a new role can highlight the need to understand a new organizational system. Often on first joining an organization, there is clear recognition of the need to Read the new context, but this tends to fade with familiarity. Equally, what is being Carried varies from situation to situation.

Carrying defensiveness in a situation will have a very different impact on consequent behavior from Carrying a feeling of confidence. The skill lies in inner attention as events unfold and reflecting on how the inner state resonates with past experience or is related to the current situation.

The two dimensions of Reading and Carrying are intricately linked: for example, if an initial assessment of the mood of a meeting is hostility to your proposal, this may lead to defensiveness in expectation of attack.

Putting the two dimensions together we posited four behavioral options.

James and Arroba (2005)

Some researchers believe that organizational politics has an impact on decision making and is threatening to an organization's effectiveness. I firmly believe, though, that it's *not* embracing politics that is more of a threat to business, as deals are lost, and talent walks out the door, taking their ideas with them (Kacmar *et al.* 1999). Ignoring politics is worse, resulting in an atmosphere of powerlessness, slowing decision making, and breeding over-controlling behaviors, which ultimately stall effectiveness. Kanter (2010) posits the view that this malaise rests mainly with middle management—which makes up the majority of the organization.

Managers need to be smart enough to read the context of the situation or work environment and reframe it. It is extremely important to grasp the nuances and less-obvious elements of the organization, and use this knowledge to make intelligent decisions on how to act—or not act.

The two dimensions taken in conjunction with the four quadrants of the Baddeley and James model enable us to understand more clearly how and why at different times and in different circumstances we are all capable of displaying different political behaviors, as illustrated in the following case study.

Eugene's Story

I was recently asked by a Singapore-based global logistics company to coach Eugene, who had been with them for about six months. Eugene constantly struggled to get his ideas sold. He worked for Terry, a dynamic and aggressive sales VP with a "what's-in-it-for-me?" attitude. Coming from an auditing background, Eugene had a strong sense of right and wrong, and felt that Terry frequently bent the rules too far in order to win accounts.

Eugene had an idea for a new sales channel that would reduce the amount of time sales staff would spend in the field and very likely give the company a higher return within 18 months. Listening to Eugene's pitch, Terry said, "Leave it with me, I'll speak with the global head of sales on this one." Months went by and nothing happened. When Eugene inquired as to progress, Terry said, "I'm with you on this one but when I presented it to the senior team, they were not keen to take it on. The bottom line is that your proposal reduces travel and expense budgets—which is great—but it cuts into everyone's livelihood and routine. They want to know what's in it for them. And frankly, I can't tell them."

Eugene couldn't believe what he was hearing. "What's in it for *them*? How about, what's in it for the company?" he thought. After reviewing expenses for the division, he decided much of the spending was fluff, and resulted in marginal sales returns. He concluded that sales did not need to do as much regional travel as it was currently clocking up, nor the high expense reports of taking clients to pricey restaurants and after-dinner entertainment. He felt this excessive spending was bordering on the unethical. His idea would reduce costs significantly and he believed the CEO would want to hear his plan. He approached Terry again and was pleasantly surprised when Terry said, "Fair enough. I think you're in a better position to take this forward. At this point it's not wise for me to step in, as you've done your homework, and I respect the effort you've put in. I actually share your thinking, and am with you. Go for it and we'll get it done." Encouraged by Terry's positive comments, Eugene immediately went to the regional SVP. He fell flat on his face. Nothing had changed and Eugene was made a pariah within the sales team. Rarely invited to meetings, he sat at his desk, travelled less, worked long hours and was relegated to completing Excel spread sheets on sales forecasts for the region. Terry no longer talked to him, and his wings had been clipped.

What can we make of this situation in light of the Baddeley–James model? Eugene was clearly naive in thinking that everyone saw the world the same way he did. He did not check in with others, did not know how the organization worked and had no allies. In this, he did not act like an Owl. He had no idea who had power or who was able to influence a change in the sales process. His confidence that Terry shared his thinking was misplaced. Had Terry been a less self-centered manager, he could have helped Eugene figure out the lay of the land, the pitfalls and the areas of resistance to his idea, and stepped in with a more logical, more thoughtful and more strategic approach. Working to solve the problem together would have moved Terry into the Owl's space and both the organization and the individual would have succeeded.

Although Eugene might be seen by some as something of a true-blue corporate person who has been wronged, it should be mentioned here that he had personal motives that drove his idea. Eugene had recently married and wanted to reduce the number of trips that kept him away from home each month. He was also quietly ambitious and resented it when other sales managers were promoted for no apparent reason. Knowing this may alter initial perceptions somewhat.

On the Baddeley–James model, Eugene's behavior was somewhere between the Donkey and the Sheep. He didn't read the power dynamics inside the organization, nor saw this element as significant. He was principled but saw everything in black and white. He failed to read the culture within the company. He had no time for the behavior of those who did not share his views and, over time, alienated himself from them to the point where they deliberately avoided attending meetings he chaired.

The end result was that everybody lost out: Eugene was sidelined and resentful; Terry was left to manage a once-vibrant sales team that was now demoralized; and, as the financial bottom line testified, the company suffered the consequences.

> Culture is . . . integral to the skill of reading that results in one being high or low in a particular context on political awareness.
>
> (James 2010)

Understanding the dynamic and holistic frame of the model, consider both the organization and individual before you embark on any project large or small. Before you pitch a new idea to your boss, ask yourself what's going on inside the organization and where your boss or the stakeholders are likely to be positioned on the particular issue at that moment. What are you reading and carrying into the situation?

Culture—both local and corporate—plays an important role in all of this. As organizations expand globally, cross-cultural dynamics present many challenges for managers and overlaying political awareness on top brings other levels of complexity. Chairing a meeting in Japan as a relatively junior manager requires a whole different approach from that which might be taken in, say, the United States, Australia or Europe. Likewise, self-promotion too is played out differently in China than in North America or India. Similarly, organizational cultures are vastly different. Therefore reading and carrying behaviors from one organization to another will be different. For example, General Electric is more used to candid, frank feedback, whereas Disney and other entertainment organizations use a less direct style of communication, one that is more nuanced and steeped in relationships. Managers joining Disney from General Electric (or vice versa) either learn this quickly or fail miserably in the process.

Politics provides a completely different frame and one that needs to be learned to ensure organizations keep talent, as the following example illustrates.

Rebecca's Story

A few years ago, I worked with an incredibly intelligent business strategist, Rebecca, a Harvard graduate. Her bosses found her brilliant: she was, they said, "99.9 percent correct on every spreadsheet for every deal," and she had phenomenal market knowledge. When a deal was in the works, she worked around the clock to make it happen, sometimes sleeping in the office over the weekend to ensure the analysis was complete before

(continued)

the meetings. The problem was that, for all her technical brilliance and hard work, Rebecca had little skill in reading situations where other people were involved. She was lucky, though, to have a boss who looked out for her. When she ruffled feathers, Matt always stepped in. Exasperated by the constant complaints about Rebecca's management style, he brought in a coach to help. Rebecca flatly refused to cooperate. Coming from middle America, she equated coaching with psychological problems, and that, of course, wasn't her. She thought her peers ("dimwits" was how she often referred to them) needed more help than she did. She told Matt to save his money or let the coach work with others in the department. Matt saw her genius, but found it increasingly difficult and time-consuming to support her. Despite her brilliance and work ethic, he had to ask Rebecca to move on. She's now with another firm and doing exactly the same thing.

A coach may have been able to help Rebecca, but only if she had accepted the need to correct her thinking, and focus on reading the nuances that are at play within every organization. As Baddely and James (1987) remind us "the four types of behavior—innocent, inept, clever, and wise—which an individual may adopt in different situations . . . are not fixed traits" and may be brought to bear to different degrees depending on the specific circumstances.

For those who still view politics from a negative perspective, the idea of thinking about reading and carrying is hard to digest. I've worked with numerous managers who are neither aware of nor choose to accept these behaviors at work. Political and situational awareness is played out daily within organizations, and using this model provides insight and helps make sense of organizational dynamics, depending on which side of the fence you sit.

Some managers believe it is much better working from the perspective of a Sheep or a Donkey—the politically unaware. Such people, whom Baddeley and James refer to as the political innocent, are unwilling to accept the organization as a political entity. If you operate in the politically unaware frame, or your boss is in this quadrant, learn how to promote your boss and team or you and the team will be unrecognized. There *are* such things as powerful functions or departments, and if you're not in one, fight for the resources to move up, or you'll be among the first in the queue for the chopping block during a downturn or a merger.

Eddie's Story

Eddie was an incredibly gifted marketing executive and always impeccably dressed. Eurasian, he was raised in Hong Kong and schooled in London. He had a PhD in research methodology and an impressive resume, having worked for global brands in the UK, Australia, Singapore and China. With a reserved and thoughtful manner, Eddie was fluent in English, Mandarin and French.

Although dressed for success, Eddie wasn't a powerhouse when he entered a room. Indeed, you wouldn't necessarily know Eddie was *in* the room until he spoke. Understated when he did speak up, he was nevertheless extremely knowledgeable in statistics and incredibly intuitive on market trends.

Eddie had recently joined a Hong Kong-based luxury goods company as the head of Consumer Insights for Asia Pacific. The company was desperate to enter China and needed a multilingual executive with strong market-research experience for the North Asia market. Eddie fit the bill.

Unhappy in his previous company—where he had worked 15-hour days, travelled globally, and had never gotten promoted—he had been looking for a change of pace and had jumped at the new job opportunity.

Soon after joining, Eddie developed a strategy for building a private label in China, which would later cover other emerging

(continued)

Asian markets. If executed properly, this strategy would easily provide multimillion-dollar returns. However, immediately after his initial research, the company underwent a major restructuring, during which the person who had hired him left, along with other senior management.

When the dust settled, he was reassigned to work under the VP of Marketing, effectively a diminution of his role. His new boss, Simon, was charismatic, well-respected, and self-obsessed. Six feet tall and neatly groomed, Simon always had a winning smile and was very adept at the art of the backhanded compliment. He did not, however, possess Eddie's educational pedigree. He regularly sparred with Henry, the head of business in Southeast Asia. At meetings, Simon usually spoke up or presented first, outlining brand positions in each market. He was good, and smooth in his delivery. He always deferred to Henry on Southeast Asian matters, however.

Simon's career goal was to relocate back to the UK and lead one of the company's branded products. He was particularly skillful at self-promotion, a keen networker, and knew how to name-drop artfully without appearing overly cloying. The carpet from his office to the new MD's office was well worn.

Simon always seemed to find an opportunity to mention the CEO's name. He had worked under her when she was the head of Research and Consumer Insights, and they had remained connected over the years. This relationship was now paying dividends. When she was in town, he was always seated next to her at dinner; at speaking events he was the one who introduced her to the dais; and he was the one that accompanied her around the region.

Simon had a gift for making himself visible at every meeting, sitting at the head of the table, next to the power. To some he was charming and smart; others thought him vapid and obvious and wondered why no-one saw through this sycophancy; but he continued to advance his career.

Under Simon's leadership, Eddie soon became less noticeable. Eddie liked Simon, enjoyed his jokes, and believed he was looking out for his interests. Eddie was extremely competent and liked to work autonomously, seldom asking Simon for advice or assistance. And as his project was moving forward with no obstacles, he saw no need to bother Simon.

Eddie had been lured away from his previous firm with a very rich package—sign-on bonus, stocks and other sweeteners—at a time when the company needed experts in China and senior Asian talent.

Simon had been with the company for 13 years, and was on an expatriate package with all the perks that came with having to move from London to Hong Kong. While he liked Eddie, he didn't like the fact that Eddie's base salary was close to his own.

Simon was a brand manager through and through. He had won brand awards and spent a great deal of money on brand campaigns. He believed the company should focus on its top product and forget private labels. Simon did not know the China consumer and had only a cursory knowledge of Eddie's project. Eddie, on the other hand, knew the market extremely well. Focusing on his research, he believed that Simon knew what he was working on.

When, after Eddie had been with the company for some six months, the new Managing Director asked everyone on the management team to review budgets with a view to cutting costs, Simon took every opportunity to undermine Eddie's project. Not only would this make him look good in the MD's eyes by cutting costs, it would also serve him well in his ongoing rivalry with the equally ambitious and equally ruthless Henry, with whom he was vying for a position in Europe. Henry, too, for his own reasons was also trying to undermine Eddie's project, in the belief that its failure would reflect badly on Simon.

Unaware of the various maneuverings going on around him, Eddie continued to work hard on the project, becoming increasingly mired in the details of packaging and interacting less with others outside the function or elsewhere in the region.

(continued)

> Knowing of the money-making potential of Eddie's project and aware of the potentially damaging battle of egos that was going on around it, some of Eddie's colleagues suggested that he stop focusing on the details and start *promoting* the project to the MD and managers in other countries who would benefit from it. Eddie's response was simply to say that everyone knew about the project already and that Simon was pushing it through. Sadly, he had no idea that at this point his name was already on the redundancy list.

What is clear from this example, apart from his seeming lack of awareness of the political infighting going on around him, was Eddie's inability or unwillingness to promote himself or his project in the proper way. Even allowing for the excesses of the Simons of this world, self-promotion shouldn't be viewed in a negative light. It is *how* you promote yourself that makes all the difference. You have to promote with *accuracy, authenticity* and *consistency*. If self-promotion goes over the edge, disregarding the team or the people around you and lacking any substance or validity, then it's the ugly and destructive side of politics.

Had Eddie been a little more politically savvy he might have developed a communication strategy that would position him and his project in a favorable light.

He could have done the following, for example:

- Created a stakeholder map of everyone connected with the project.
- Crafted an email discussing the scope, implications, benefits and risks of the project.
- Provided presentations, either face-to-face or through webinars.
- Ensured that a broader audience, beyond marketing and China, was kept up to date.

The benefits to such a communication strategy are many. He would have established himself more widely and more clearly as an expert in his field and been able to share his expertise with a broader audience, including the CEO. In the process, he would have created a buzz within and beyond the organization, which would have reflected well on his boss.

I'm often asked "What if my boss doesn't like me doing this?" or "How can I go around my boss?" or "I work for a narcissistic boss that wants to win and takes no prisoners. How do I promote my work under these conditions?" Clearly it's unwise to go around your boss; they must be kept in the communication loop. If you work for someone like Simon (overly ambitious and not thrilled with being out of the limelight), you must be able to understand their motivation and demonstrate what's in it for them. Interestingly enough, the narcissist is much easier to manage than the depraved bully or the inept politician. Visibility benefits everyone, particularly your boss, and even more so if your boss is like Simon.

If Eddie had sent the email out to a global distribution network, Simon would have shared the benefits. The end result: Eddie would have owned the project, received recognition, and everyone would have known his name, making it difficult to put him on any redundancy list. It would have been political suicide for Simon to continue with the campaign against him. Had he done these things, Eddie would probably have remained at the company and be viewed (rightfully) as a high-potential talent with great prospects for promotion.

AUTHENTIC SELF-PROMOTION

Many people, all over the world, don't like to engage in politics and are unaware of how to do so while holding onto their values. I've researched, interviewed and delivered workshops with professionals in Europe, North America and Asia and always hear the following: "I'm Chinese/Singaporean/Indian/French/British/Canadian and we don't talk about accomplishments."

Across the Asia Pacific region, a recurring comment—especially from women—is: "I was taught to be modest and to not brag about my achievements."

But consider the consequences of not being savvy and not finding your voice. Your career stalls, your ideas get lost or, worse, are stolen, and disillusion soon sets in. Many leave to join another firm, hoping things will be "less political." But that never really happens—the same issues resurface. How could they not? People are not fundamentally different from company to company. And you're likely to repeat the same behavior and revisit the same scenarios until you learn. Unlike eternal purgatory, you *can* move ahead. There is such a thing as authentic self-promotion.

In addition to sending emails to your stakeholders, authentic self-promotion might include starting a blog, publishing an article, or being seen in the media—in print, on the internet or on television.

In my talks or workshops, one person in the audience will inevitably ask a question about the Myers-Briggs preference for introversion. Typical comments include: "I'm an introvert, I don't like to talk about what I do and I don't like to network," or "Have you worked with other executives who are shy and have found ways to overcome their shyness?"

For such people, the best approach is to do what comes naturally: one-on-one meetings or smaller-group discussions to share what they are working on. Another approach is to use technology (email or blog posts) to share information about you and your team's accomplishments, highlighting how this achievement has an impact on the organization and applications for learning. When attending a conference, take time to connect with one or two people; feel confident that you don't need to walk away with a handful of business cards or connections. Share your insights with a small group of colleagues at a lunch or at a meeting. Keep the group small and provide advice that is factual and that will have an impact.

ENDNOTES

1. A business-focused social media site (www.linkedin.com) that enables professionals to make contacts and connections.
2. Rhymer Rigby, "Don't forget your PQ: your power/political quotient," *Financial Times*, September 20, 2010.
3. While the authors ascribe specific characteristics to the various animals, it's worth bearing in mind that different cultures attach different connotations to the animals depicted in the model.
4. In regular email correspondence with James and Baddeley during the writing of this book in 2010.

CHAPTER 3

Surviving the Ebbs and Flows of Power

Nancy's Story

Nancy, Vice President of Human Resources for a global consumer-products firm, caught the morning flight to New York from London. In her laptop was a clearly constructed strategy for an HR function she believed would catapult her career to the next level.

Nancy reported to Janice, the Executive Vice President of Human Resources. They had worked together for many years and were well known as frequent speakers at prominent global HR conferences.

Janice believed that Nancy knew more on European HR practices than anyone in the market and considered her a loyal and dedicated employee. Outside of work, they were also good friends and spent a good deal of time discussing the intricate details of a large restructuring project that was being introduced across the company. Up until that time, HR had been a

(continued)

centralized function, focusing entirely on policy, compensation and development and Nancy had devoted herself to building a solid team of HR professionals, driving engagement through cultural-change projects and designing a program for high-potential staff.

Some executives viewed HR very differently, however. To them, HR was bureaucratic and over-staffed. It added little value to the bottom line and was thus in need of restructuring.

Nancy had watched and waited to gauge which way the winds of change were blowing, and believed the time was now right to present her plan. In her 10 years with the company, she had shown herself to be an astute observer of people and dynamics. By doing what was expected of her, she had risen steadily, though by no means spectacularly, under Janice's leadership. Though well regarded in HR circles, elsewhere in the company Nancy was seen as being conservative in dress, reserved and aloof in manner, and not always approachable.

Under the recent changes, the company had changed its approach to the market, restructuring around geographies. Corporate headquarters relocated to New York and regional offices remained in London, Sao Paolo, and Hong Kong. The restructuring meant that Human Resources now reported directly to the business heads. For the first time in her career Nancy would report to a business leader, Michael, a new Executive VP known as a turnaround expert and renowned as a powerful, charismatic leader.

Throughout Nancy's entire career in Human Resources she had supported and followed a powerful leader. She began as a payroll clerk, moved through various HR disciplines and finally made it to the corner office overlooking the River Thames. Nancy worked well with a few people and managed others at a distance. She had few friends outside of work, preferring her own company, reading and gardening. After a bout of serious illness, she became a strict vegan and let everyone know about it. Nancy was close to six feet tall and it was this that gave her a certain presence. She was very thin, reserved and rarely smiled. She appeared calm but had a less-than-tolerant side, particularly with waiters, clerks and airline personnel. She had little patience for mistakes, and treated with derision any members of staff that failed to meet her exacting standards. Nevertheless, Nancy believed she was well liked and she always worked well with senior management, who never saw that side of her behavior.

When Nancy was promoted to VP, Janice provided her with executive coaching to help with the transition and smooth out her rough edges. While Nancy didn't believe that she had problems with her staff, she introduced some of her own practices into the workplace. Sensing that everyone was on high alert during the merger and reorganization, she started classes in yoga, nutrition and health to reduce stress and find a more even work-life balance.

One of Nancy's biggest challenges was voice and presence. She had a tendency to speak softly and to swallow her words at the end of a sentence. In meetings, she was often asked to "speak up" and, Janice noticed, was often overruled or completely ignored when presenting new ideas. While Nancy knew she needed to work on this, she also felt being British in an American firm didn't help. "If I don't get the job it's because I have the wrong accent. You have to be American to get ahead around here," she told one of her colleagues.

When it came to dress, the conversation took a different turn. Nancy didn't believe in pretense, and preferred a natural look over a made-up face. In HR circles, Janice was Chanel and Nancy was J Crew. When Janice hired personal-grooming coaches for her team, Nancy thought this ridiculous, but participated in the sessions anyhow. She had no plans to spend outrageous sums on clothes, but greatly enjoyed the workshop on colors, from which she became convinced that pastel colors gave her energy. From that day on, she wore pink, yellow and purple pant suits.

Before Nancy flew out of London, a colleague, Maria, came up to warn her about Michael. "He is one of those executives that will size you up in one minute," she said. "You're either in or out.

(continued)

It's that quick. And you need to look the part too–*appearance matters* with this guy," she emphasized.

Nancy took these remarks in her stride and didn't think any executive could be that superficial. She came from humble beginnings, believed in substance over style and thought all the talk on what to wear went out of fashion in the 1980s, along with shoulder pads and killer pumps. So, while she had thanked Maria for the advice, she was quietly confident that she could handle whatever came her way. She had always worked hard and believed in substance over fluff; the rest didn't really matter. While dress was important, she didn't believe Armani suits and Gucci loafers could make or break a career, and dismissed such thinking as simple-minded. She'd made it this far without all the trappings and wasn't going to change now. She was ambitious, nevertheless, and so, in deference to her colleague's comments, she purchased a lilac linen suit from Talbots. Lilac, she believed, provided energy, and was a good color on her.

Nancy arrived at the corporate offices overlooking Central Park just before noon. Stepping off the elevator on the 38th floor, she was met by two assistants; both wore Chanel suits and high heels, and had perfectly manicured nails. For reasons she could not quite put into words, Nancy felt a little uncomfortable. The senior of the two assistants gave Nancy a brief appraising look and said: "Michael's running late. He's just finishing up a conference call with the CEO," and motioned her towards a plush leather seat to wait. Declining an offer of coffee from the junior assistant, and with growing unease, Nancy sat down to wait, wondering how, if the company was undergoing cost savings, it could afford this office and *two* assistants.

When she was finally ushered into Michael's office, she was somewhat taken aback by his relaxed demeanor as he welcomed with an offer of a cup of organic green tea. He seemed nice; not the egocentric leader others had made him out to be. He was over six feet tall, with short, jet-black gelled hair and a chiseled chin. He wore black slacks, a T-shirt, soft leather loafers and, she noticed, no socks. A black Armani jacket was draped over the leopard-skin chair. As she glanced around, she noticed that an entire wall was covered with family photos, of Michael winning races, of Michael shaking hands with celebrities and sports stars. A surfboard hung on the other wall and in the middle of the office was a hand-crafted, highly polished, Colnago-designed racing bike. Clearly, this was a man who had achieved much and who was proud of his achievements. At age 40, he was Executive Vice President of a major global brand, a seasoned triathlete, and a father of three. Though new to the company, he had had extensive experience in the industry. Originally from California, he had relocated his family to New York for this role.

Michael came from money. He had been to the best schools, was well travelled and spoke French fluently. He did not shy away from publicity, was frequently quoted in the press, and enjoyed dining with sports figures and celebrities. He valued intelligence, looks, dress, and all the trappings. Michael appeared friendly but perhaps a little distant, Nancy thought; probably preoccupied with the recent conference call with the CEO.

With her usual attention to detail, Nancy had spent an inordinate amount of time developing the business case to combine the international HR function and believed that the restructuring would secure her position in the role. Europe, after all, was the largest market and she was currently the VP in charge. She had already begun to increase resources across Europe, particularly in HR, and was looking to Asia for the cost-cutting that Michael wanted.

Yet Nancy's reputation had preceded her. While Michael was aware of her record and legendary attention to detail, he had also heard about Nancy's treatment of staff and her quirky new-age programs. He recognized ambition when he saw it but his focus was on business, efficiencies and cutting costs. He intended to rebuild Asia and Europe by reducing headcount and bringing in high-potential, highly compensated talent. He also planned huge investments in technology, to create efficiencies and reduce bureaucracy.

(continued)

Nancy began her presentation by expressing the view that there was a need to increase headcount to meet the increasing reporting requirements demanded by corporate headquarters. To ask more of her staff, she said, would bring them into conflict with local labor laws.

Michael's response to this was simply to smile and nod as she presented her case for more resources.

But Michael, too, had done his homework and had come to a quite different conclusion. He knew the European business was losing revenue year on year and Asia had potential for significant growth. In general, he was unimpressed with HR, a department which, as he said when Nancy's presentation came to a natural pause, he considered to be "riddled with spread-sheet jockeys."

Somewhat taken aback by this comment, she realized that she had got off on the wrong foot. From that moment onwards, her presentation began to fall apart as she stumbled and stammered through the next 45 minutes. All her research into European demographics, talent projections, labor laws and HR requirements made little impression: Michael was interested only in the bottom line. By the time she had brought her case to a less-than-compelling conclusion, Michael had already summed her up as a "typical HR person." His detailed cross-examination of her case had not only confirmed this rather dismissive view but, worse, had led him also to conclude that she lacked both presence and leadership.

As he walked her out of his office, Michael thanked Nancy for her time and "interesting" perspectives. On hearing that one little adjective, she knew then that the plan she had once thought of as airtight was doomed to failure. Had she been feeling any less devastated as she walked towards the elevator, she might have paid more attention to the young man who headed the company's HR activities in Asia, who was being ushered into Michael's office with a warm handshake and a sniggering comment that invited the visitor to share the Executive VP's amusement about "what *she* was wearing."

In this example, Nancy ran into one of the biggest challenges executives face: the ever-changing nature of the business landscape, for which the majority are inadequately prepared. Few business schools have modules dedicated to teaching how to survive corporate restructuring, new leadership, and radical change. Within many organizations, too, the focus tends to be on the soft, emotional side of change management, or the very detailed planning side of change, rarely delving into the hard-boiled political side of resistance.

All change projects or mergers and acquisitions are accompanied by power shifts which change the political landscape. To survive, you must embrace that change. This requires active monitoring of the underlying organizational shifts. Simply keeping your head down and hoping that the chaos will soon blow over is naive: it won't. Everyone needs to embrace the political landscapes and engage with opposing factions to understand the subtle sabotage that takes place during upheaval. Don't shrink away from the hard stuff—stay alert. Buchanan (2008) observes that "power, politics and change are inextricably linked" and that political maneuverings increase during times of change. Everyone fights for scarce resources and jostles for position; change quickly exaggerates and drives political behavior.

During periods of change, visibility supersedes ability, and being visible often has a way of building credibility. Although much of this swirls around self-promotion, as we have seen already, there are subtle and not-so-subtle ways of going about it. While the subtle approach often works better, you need to turn up the volume to get noticed. People are focused on their own issues, and may not hear you unless it is loud enough.

Managers can often find themselves on the wrong side of the tracks during times of change. In our scenario above, Nancy was the one to suffer. It should be noted, though, that under other circumstances Michael too could be equally vulnerable.

Mergers, acquisitions and large-scale change projects bring out the best (and worst) in political behavior. Organizational Development professionals, business leaders, scholars and authors continue to write books and build consulting hours around change management. There are stacks of books and mountains of research from global think-tanks on why mergers fail.[1] Why can't organizations ever get it right?

Human nature dictates that any change or merger is bound to meet with resistance, but this is not the most significant component contributing to the failure of so many change programs. Resistance is often very obvious and therefore more easily combatted. The real difficulty with change or mergers comes from the more subtle undermining of the process through the informal maneuverings and lobbying of power networks within organizations.

When Nancy heard whispers of a restructuring, her political antennae were up, but she missed some important elements. When change occurs, typically everyone panics, turf battles increase, power shifts constantly and everyone is out for themselves. This is politics with an edge. It's palpable, and the naive few who fail to heed and respond to the signs had better look out.

Nancy saw early on what was happening and felt the need to fight for resources in her market. She also saw change as a way forward in her career. Unfortunately for her, Michael had different ideas and Michael clearly had the power to get what he wanted. Outside of Janice, Nancy had little support or protection. She knew where she wanted to be but she made mistakes and her plan failed to get her there.

We have to ask ourselves, then, what Nancy could have done differently. There are a number of things that she should have known to ensure that her plan had the greatest chance of succeeding.

1. **Understanding power and negotiating shifts**: Nancy didn't know her new boss and didn't have a sufficiently strong network in place to enable her to navigate through the transition. Her career strategy had been based on one person, Janice, and she'd had

little interaction with other key stakeholders. Her first step should have been to find out more about her new boss, Michael. She'd heard about Michael's reputation as a "turnaround expert" but as that was the only information she had, she had very little knowledge on which to base her proposal. As would be expected of someone in his position, Michael had developed the plan long before Nancy arrived. The chances are that he would have had others working on it with him. Nancy should have tapped into this group to have a better understanding about the strategy and to learn more about Michael and his working style.

Prior to Michael's appointment, Nancy's network which she could tap into for advice, feedback and support was extremely narrow, and one that Michael didn't care for. Had she been a little more savvy, she would have known how important reputation is and how crucial it is to manage it properly. When Michael tapped into the business community for feedback on the work of HR, what he heard added further fuel to his already negative thoughts. Had Nancy been more connected, she could have managed this perception. Indeed, she should have been part of Michael's team and perhaps would have been had it not been for the reputation that she and the HR department had acquired for themselves. She needed to network and connect with influential opinion leaders outside of the HR function.

2. **Dress the part**: Nancy's colleagues and boss had invested time in helping prepare her for an executive role. Many of us don't have this luxury. You wouldn't go to Nike in a suit and you can't visit Chanel without one. It's as simple as that.

As my son's high school teacher told her class, "First impressions are lethal." It is awful to say, but people—both men and women—are sized up in seconds. The look is about fit, and fit is about culture. Many organizations hire for cultural fit. Dress may be thought to be a minor part, as long as you have "nice clothes" on, but often plays a significant role. It's not only dress that counts, though; it's the whole package. In the case of Frank in Chapter 1, for example, the company looked beyond outward appearance at what else Frank brought to the arrangement. In this case, however, Nancy's presentation, language and voice all counted against her. Consciously or not, we all make judgments about others on such things on a daily basis. It is something we do spontaneously, naturally and continuously. And, rightly or wrongly, "not only are reputations and first impressions formed quickly, they are durable" (Pfeffer 2010). It is therefore necessary to be alert to the rules, stated or otherwise, that inform the culture of your specific workplace.

Robert's Story

Robert, SVP of Global Operations for a large multinational consumer-goods company, had joined the company two years ago, having come from a prestigious ad agency. He was the consummate sales person: gregarious and street smart. Watching industry trends, he saw the market shifting and believed the company would be in a better position if more autonomy was given to country managers. Working with a strategic consulting firm he had tested and proved his hypothesis to be sound. With the support of his boss, Richard, he was able to convince the CEO of the need to move away from a centralized structure and place product design and responsibility with the country heads in growth markets in Asia, Europe and Latin America. He sold the idea on the basis of cost savings and productivity growth, which he believed would benefit everyone. But to be successful, the change would need perfect execution which, in turn, relied upon cultural understanding and high sensitivity to local politics.

Robert organized a series of conference calls, which involved Richard and the CEO, to spread the word with the global executive teams. Under the new structure, reporting lines would change and power would be redistributed. To no-one's surprise, not everyone was happy with this; particularly

Francisco, SVP of Operations, a company veteran who had worked his way up from brand manager in Latin America to overseeing Asia and Middle East, the second-most profitable division.

In preparing for the change, Robert met with all executives to ensure alliances and gain their support. Francisco and others gave the nod but saw things differently. With Richard at his side, Robert spent months furiously trying to galvanize the newly structured teams on the new way of working. Robert believed the best angle to drive change was to make the business case forcefully and run with it. And run they did. The CEO was in on every conference call. Robert knew how to appeal to authority and used power to drive the change forward. What he hadn't realized, however, was the extent to which the organization was driven by relationships.

Robert hadn't read the organization correctly. *It was not ready* for such a radical overhaul, but Robert was too caught up with the big-picture view to know this. Richard actually knew the challenges much better, and could clearly see the pending turf battles. Richard, however, was close to retirement: not wanting to lose his pension over this one, he decided it was best to say little and let Robert fight the good fight.

Second, Robert underestimated the value and impact of relationships and, more importantly, ignored the hidden power bases.

During the conference calls, Francisco sat back and listened while others vented their anger over the proposals. Between calls, he used this resistance—and his close, long-standing relationship with the CEO—to build a new structure of his own. Suspicious of Robert's motivations, and seeing this relative newcomer as a politician with aspirations for the CEO's role, Francisco put more resources in the markets and restructured his corporate team around centers of excellence. He had both the power and "moral" authority within the company and knew

(continued)

its culture; he also knew the products, had the respect of his peers, and controlled revenue.

As Robert did not assess the power bases as clearly as he should have, it was not until months later that he began to see what was happening. In the face of this quiet resistance, Robert's project had started to disintegrate, and over the following six months slowly started to return to its original structure. By then, it was too late to reverse the flow. Jobs were lost in the process, depriving the organization of some of its top talent and Robert of his influence.

As mentioned earlier, there's plenty of research into why mergers fail or why change doesn't work, and many times it is linked clearly to a failure to anticipate and deal with cultural obstacles and power bases. Mapping the political landscape is the only guarantor for success. As organizational change unfolds, jockeying for position and turf protection noticeably increase. In the case study above, Francisco saw that the restructuring would have significant impact on his function, shifting resources and, ultimately, power to Robert. As tensions amplified, talented employees who were uneasy about the long-term outcome started answering the calls of search firms and eventually left the company.

While many textbooks advocate appointing a leader to manage the M&A project, this never eliminates the behind-the-scenes maneuvering and power struggles within the executive or management ranks. In this particular case, there were two political forces underpinning this turn of events: Francisco, who was not involved in the restructuring and who disliked Robert intensely; and Robert, who though ambitious and street smart, missed the opportunity to drive a restructuring that would have benefitted the organization on many levels. He failed to recognize Francisco's concerns. A basic element in any negotiation is understanding, in depth, your opponent's concerns. This political misunderstanding harks back to Hobbes's observation on politics that men often oppose a thing merely because they have no agency or planning in it" (Kaplan 2002). The macro forces shaping change were not enough to drive this restructure. The bottom line here is that Robert failed to evaluate completely the political force and power source operating within the organization.[2]

Anyone who has participated in a merger or acquisition, gone through a leadership change, or worked through a large-scale change project has seen politics in play, although this may not always be seen for what it is. Before a merger, change or leadership shift, those best able to navigate their way through potentially troubled waters and use the tide to their advantage are those who have:

- A good understanding of politics at play
- A thorough awareness of power dynamics
- A detailed list of stakeholders and a map of power networks
- A plan of action and requisite influence strategies.

I've watched many great managers drive mergers and acquisitions and then leave the organization once the project ended. Most didn't have a network in place, had no awareness of power or, worse, managed to aggravate influential stakeholders in the process. They were focused on driving the change and completing the task but overlooked the subtle side of change—power shifts and networks.

Long before the merger talks begin, you must have your network in place and keep a close watch on power shifts inside the organization. More importantly, safeguard your own position by ensuring that other people know what you are doing. Change-management texts reiterate the strategic value of communication during change, but it's really all about self-promotion. Talk about what you're doing openly and frequently and make certain you're sharing this information with those in power.

ENDNOTE

1. See, for example, Rick Maurer's web-based *Change Without Migraines* series.

CHAPTER 4

Taking Things at Face Value: Trust, But Verify

Scholars and management consultants talk about organizations as political systems and frames. Legitimate, factual and positive politics is a critical component of organizational life.

Everybody in a company is part of a politically organized community, a polity, and each person's role and behavior in that polity is determined by his or her inherited nature, up-bringing and training.

(Tuck and Earl 1996)

Though many are reluctant to discuss politics and power within organizations, it is undeniable that they co-exist in the workplace. Whenever there is more than one person in a room, politics exists, and we ignore this at our peril. Having a healthy approach to and appreciation for politics and power drives innovation and enables companies to retain their best talent. It's a very simple concept but it works.

A company is a community of people with established norms and behaviors on how to work. To fit in, people act according to what they believe are the rules of group behavior. But there's more to company life than simply being aware of the rules: being savvy is having a sixth sense about what's *really* going on in the spaces in between.

Various scholars have equated the term "savvy" with a sharp intellect and healthy dose of wisdom and craftiness (see, Tuck and Earl 1996, for example).

While we may all recognize structures, policies and procedures, many of us do not take power and influence networks, into consideration, giving scant thought to the idea that some interactions and messages might be hidden. Rose-colored glasses may be useful sometimes, but at work consider wearing a different pair.

Change your frame of reference and start to see organizations as political systems; a legitimate, factual and positive work environment.

Do you see things for what they are or fail to see the gentle nuances, power struggles and maneuverings around you? Here are a few questions you can ask yourself to sharpen the focus:

- Why is this person telling me this?
- What's the underlying motivation?
- How am I looking at this picture?
- What's missing?

Any emotion—anger, happiness, sadness or relief—is generated by a particular set of circumstances, so you need to examine it. When things go awry, don't be content to simply write it off as someone "having a bad day" or put their behavior down to forgetfulness. The excuses continue until someone leaves the organization.

Throughout this book, I argue that power and politics are necessary elements of organizational life. Managers who are blind to the social and political dynamics sooner or later find themselves pushed aside.

Entering organizational life, managers need to be equipped with specific business skills, but there is more. They need political awareness. Some organizations mistake the savvy skills highlighted in this book with emotional quotient (EQ). While there may be a slight overlap between the two, savvy is quite different. I've worked with many managers who are strong in EQ but lack the street-smart knowledge that will take their career to the next level or help sell an idea. The EQ review used by many independent consulting groups has an Emotional Competence Inventory focusing on organizational awareness, which many define as "reading the emotional currents and power relationships."[1] While this is critical, most EQ management programs from the EQ assessment focus on developing empathy rather than building savvy awareness. *Both* are necessary. Anyone with management aspirations requires a solid grounding in political intelligence and relationships.

Robert Sutton, professor of management science and engineering at Stanford University, has written extensively on the seamier side of the social dynamics of organizational life: the corporate bully; the mean-spirited individual who controls through fear; the overly political, self-absorbed, arrogant boss or colleague.

But what about the subtle side of politics? This is the side many of us don't see or refuse to see—the overly nice politician that may or may not have your back covered; the fair-weather manager that flows with the organizational tide, and when the currents shift you're alone on deck. This category also includes the person you

> . . . too many managers are either naive or cynical about organizational politics.
>
> (Bohman and Deal 2008)

may dismiss as overly political, but who nevertheless conveys important messages, whispers, and hints that may prove critical to your future. In other words, we need to distinguish those who are potential allies as well as potential adversaries, including the "what's good for me, works for you" type of colleague.

When first joining an organization you may start with a desk, a computer and policy manuals, but no one tells you the rules. You have obligatory meetings with your team members and depending on your role, maybe also with someone of influence or power. You're focused on doing the right thing, oblivious to subtle nuances, and think everyone is your friend. If someone upsets you, you make excuses—"They didn't mean it" or "It's just not that important." That may be the case but, then again, maybe they *did* mean it and it *is* important. Go in with your eyes wide open. Politicians of all stripes are alive and well in every organization. Everyone comes to work with baggage and they don't always check it at the door. Some carry it with them every day. Are you dealing with a core group of Owls—the positive pragmatists—or a coalition of immoral Foxes, or a narcissistic leader? Once you've

> Women are as likely as men to be exposed to organizational politics, raising questions concerning whether women perceive, use, and are affected differently by such behavior.
>
> (Buchanan 2008)

examined the core group dynamics, consider the individuals inside this group: friend, ally, adversary or antagonist? Where do they fall? More important—where are *you*? (Stybel and Peabody 2005)

Forget what you were taught in school and follow former US President Ronald Reagan's Cold War maxim: "Trust but verify."

Carly's Story

As a Vice President for a UK-based oil conglomerate, Carly had established a reputation as an expert in M&A. Her skills were in demand, both inside and outside the energy and gas industry. After a 20-year career in the corporate world, she was in need of a change. When an attractive offer came in from an organization in Hong Kong she took on the challenge.

The company was looking to integrate a smaller local organization and believed that Carly was the one to drive the integration. At the interview, the Asia Pacific head of Human Resources, Aaron, had told her that she was the "change agent" they needed "to bring in new thinking and a sense of urgency" to what he described as "essentially a conservative organization." Aaron's affable nature and open style had been the tipping point, and she jumped at the opportunity, knowing cultural integration was her strong suit.

In the first couple of months, Carly found it relatively easy to add value, as many of the existing processes were easily improved. She moved quickly and made an impact. The early wins on the integration and positive feedback from her boss were encouraging.

After she had been in the role for about three months, she was invited to lunch by Wade, the head of Marketing. Wade had been with the company for 15 years and was a shrewd student of power politics. The impression she had formed of him up to that point was that he had excellent marketing skills and was a big talker—perhaps a little too full of himself, but very well connected globally.

Over lunch, he complimented Carly on the impact her work was having on the company but intimated that it was also giving cause for concern among some regional employees, who

(continued)

were worried about the possibility of losing their jobs. He suggested that it might be useful if Carly spent some time talking to the team about the implications of the changes for their careers with the company.

Carly thanked him for his insights, but reassured him that there was always anxiety amongst staff whenever there was a merger. She had had a great deal of experience of such matters and he could be confident that she knew how to handle it, she told him.

As she was getting up to leave Wade said something that gave her pause for a moment: "With all the changes and redundancies from this merger, how long will your role be needed? Six months? A year? Think about it."

Though she laughed them off at the time as the remarks of a disgruntled man who was taking his fears out on her, Wade's questions lingered with her for weeks.

When she told Aaron of this conversation some time later, he told her not to worry. Not everyone could see the progress that was being made, but when they did everything would be fine, he reassured her. "Wade doesn't know a lot about mergers," he said, and there was something in his tone that implied that Wade was a whiner and needed to be put in his place from time to time. Aaron relied on Carly's expertise to manage the chaos and the emotional outbursts of the regional team during the merger. Though he'd been through mergers before, none had been as complicated as this one. Tempers were short as turf battles raged.

Aaron had joined the firm just eight months earlier than Carly but his introduction and integration into the firm had been far more leisurely and far more extensive than that which he'd offered to Carly. From the start, he had become familiar with the CEO and just about everyone on the executive team. When she arrived, the merger was already in full swing and there was little time for a gentle orientation and integration course. Apart from an interrupted PowerPoint presentation on corporate culture and a few sarcastic comments about HR strategy from Aaron, she had been left pretty much to her own devices. He had given her the benefit of some of his often humorous impressions of various members of the corporate hierarchy, of course, but that had been the extent of her introduction to the company.

Carly didn't mind this; each of Aaron's stories had presented another piece to the puzzle and she appreciated his rebellious sense of humor. She found his style refreshing and was excited about the upcoming projects preparing employees for the newly merged company. Though she was aware of his shortcomings with regard to integrating her into the corporate culture, she didn't quite know how to confront him about this. She contented herself with the thought that something was bound to be done about this when the dust had settled on the chaos of the merger.

Carly observed that Aaron staffed his team with relatively junior managers, and liked to pile on the work, a tactic that some believed he used to pressure those he didn't like out of the organization.

Aaron had a reputation for being a big talker and tough negotiator and was adroit at managing perceptions inside the company. He enjoyed being in the limelight and being viewed as the go-to person for HR. Though he relied heavily on Carly's expertise to re-build the HR function, he was quick to claim credit for her good ideas among the executive team and other senior colleagues. Because she shared his vision, she was a willing participant in his plans to change the HR function and to roll out processes to support the newly merged organization.

She was flattered by Aaron's recognition of her knowledge and was eager to impress her boss and add value to the organization. While she had had more experience in mergers and acquisitions, he had more experience in HR, and she believed their skill sets complemented one another and they'd make a great team. Feeling that they were working together towards the same goals, she was prepared to take work home and to put in long hours at nights and at weekends.

(continued)

Wade, however, was proving to be a thorn in everyone's side (despite the fact that Aaron spent considerable time with him), ranting about the good marketing and sales talent that was being forced to leave as a result of the reorganization. He believed that HR's energies would be better focused on career planning rather than on synergy targets and cultural integration. So loud and widespread were his remarks, that his concerns even reached the ears of those in corporate headquarters.

Carly, however, had different priorities and hoped that, as part of the restructure, Wade's position would be relocated to another region. Nevertheless, she was forced to look into his claims and found that those who had left the company were not, in fact, top talent, but mediocre performers. This fact made little difference, however, when she conveyed it to Wade and the regional team. Having to do battle on all fronts eventually took its toll on her performance and left her exhausted and open to further criticism. When Wade took the opportunity to openly question her role, Aaron did nothing to defend her and she found herself increasingly isolated.

When in one of their regular bi-weekly conference calls Carly gave a candid explanation of her position, outlining to the corporate team an elaborate transition plan, her words fell on deaf ears. Wade's voice, it seemed, was much louder than hers and his networks across the company much wider.

When, a few months later, a new Managing Director for Asia Pacific joined the team there was even greater pressure to cut costs: recruitment was frozen, salaries were cut, and bonuses and promotions postponed. Aaron, ever mindful of his own position and astute enough to know which way the wind was blowing, withdrew any remaining support he had for Carly and, as the pressure for redundancies mounted, added her name to the list of early departures.

What are we to make of all this? Is there anything that Carly could and should have done to ensure that these circumstances could never arise? Gaining a complete grasp of the complex maneuverings that take place inside organizations may never be possible, especially in the short space of time that Carly had available to her, but there are several things she could have done to make her position more secure and ensure she operated from a position of greater strength. Indeed, we would all benefit from the following steps:

1.   **Start with an in-depth plan**: A job description is often not the real measurement for a specific role. To understand the organization, the culture, the management team and her role within them, Carly needed solid connections, support, and relationships across the organization. Although Wade was high maintenance and she viewed him as a politician, he provided insights into the organization that Aaron hadn't learned or didn't know. She should have focused more on building connections, discovering networks and finding out where she stood.

2.   **Find a core group of sponsors**: Carly took Aaron at face value and never questioned his support. Rather than relying solely on him, she should have sought out a group of sponsors within the first month of being there, involving them more closely in the change process while establishing herself as the expert. Aaron proved to be a fair-weather manager, but because she was so reliant on him she had no fallback position when he withdrew his support.

3.   **Understand the real measure for the role**: To give herself any chance of succeeding, she would have had to widen her focus to decipher the complicated decision matrix and power mix. She needed to understand how the organization and the boss measured success and judged performance. Some may think her failure was from cost-cutting and restructuring. But would the outcome have been different if she had the same connections as Aaron or Wade? Before starting a new job you're given a job description, highlighting the skills and competencies needed along with expectations and measurements. But

as you move up the organization you're assessed on factors not listed in any job description. This is what Brandon and Seldman (2004) call the "real scorecard" for a role. In Carly's case, this was uncovered during her meetings with Wade and others. As she moved through the first three months, building a network along the way, the scorecard became more apparent. Her difficulty was managing the different priorities of multiple stakeholders, not only in Hong Kong but also corporate headquarters, who held different opinions and expectations for this role.

4. Be aware of the need to uncover political affiliations: Carly should have uncovered potential advocates, adversaries and antagonists from the outset. She chose not to detect or respond to the whispers and nuances of people's behavior, listening instead to Aaron and disregarding Wade, which cost her heavily.

Transitioning into a new role or organization is not easy and countless books have been written on the subject.[2] Choosing and walking the right path requires a well-thought-out plan.

The first three months is the honeymoon period; everything and everyone looks nice, friendly and well intentioned. Don't be blinded by niceness. Assess what's behind or underneath facades to uncover where power lies and how the organization operates politically. If you look and listen closely enough to informal conversations and the meaning behind the words, you'll find the kind of clues that Carly missed—Aaron's ambition and need for recognition; Wade's awareness of the bigger picture.

Anyone joining a new company or moving into a new position should think carefully about the strengths and skills that made them successful in their previous roles and whether these are sufficient to meet the demands of the new role. If you can identify the kind of support you require in the new role, who will provide this? It is equally important to know who will *not* support you.

Second, study your boss and his/her mode of operating in the political environment of the company. Make a point of finding out what motivates this person and influences their decision-making processes. What are their preferred methods of communication (email, phone, face-to-face?), their personal skills and possible hidden agendas.

You also need to understand how the business itself operates. This will entail having a clear understanding of where the real decision-making power lies.

Transitioning into a new role or organization is never easy. Bridges (2009) indicates that it is not the *change* but the *transition* that impacts managers more profoundly. Watkins (2003) and Fischer (2007) provide guidance on how to survive leadership transitions. A critical element with each transition is to understand your boss, your stakeholders and the team's political persuasion. With a new company, function or geography, you walk a tightrope of risk unless you choose the right path, which necessitates a well-thought-out plan.

> Only when you succeed in making yourself an active part of the network of relationships that exist behind the formal organizational chart do you have a realistic chance of initiating relatively big changes.
>
> (Fischer 2007)

When taking over a new team, there is little time to make an impression. Some narrow this down to a 90-day period; others, such as Manzoni and Barsoux (2009), indicate a new boss has about five days to do so. Fischer (2007) moves beyond typical scenario planning and revamps transition planning, building a holistic view to understand organizational terrain and key relationships inside and outside the firm. His focus on predecessors, legacy and supporting staff provides depth and sharpness to any transitional plan.

For Fischer, a successful transition comes from the new person's ability to differentiate him/herself from others, particularly predecessors. Yet few managers or organizations consider the role of the predecessor when designing a plan, nor create a detailed plan to include those relationships. The dynamics between newly appointed managers and their predecessors are critical for understanding the "hidden competition" (Fischer 2007) and determining smooth transitions, yet few organizations incorporate this into their transition planning.

Given the high cost of executive departures, bringing in a new executive or promoting internally requires focus and tremendously detailed planning. A critical part of this process is ensuring that new or recently promoted employees receive proper introductions to the company and the role.

A Hong Kong-based senior hire with a global luxury brand told me her first week on the job was miserable. She was hired to lead the company's PR but was not provided with a desk; for the first week she shuffled from a temporary office to a makeshift cubicle, until they finally found a place for her. The role had only recently been upgraded and her predecessor had reported to a lower-level manager. In such circumstances, moving into a new (upgraded) role can be challenging; the legacy and old stereotypes remain. The new hire needs to change perceptions as will be discussed in Chapter 6.

Fischer highlights seven building blocks for a successful transition, one of which examines the role of the predecessor. The chart shown in Figure 4.1 is a useful aid in transitioning leaders or anyone new to a role.

Each quadrant in the chart requires a different strategy, and while one may see a glorified predecessor as a continuous threat, more worrisome is the criticized predecessor, particularly one who remains with the company. This relationship needs to be carefully managed, as organizational bonds of attachment remain. Teams hold onto past relationships with the predecessor while looking for the successor to save the department, function or team.

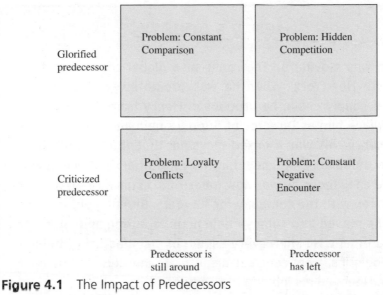

	Predecessor is still around	Predecessor has left
Glorified predecessor	Problem: Constant Comparison	Problem: Hidden Competition
Criticized predecessor	Problem: Loyalty Conflicts	Problem: Constant Negative Encounter

Figure 4.1 The Impact of Predecessors
Source: Fischer 2007

If the previous incumbent was not sufficiently political, the team will now look for more visibility, someone to pull them out of the doldrums. The new hire's first act should be to bring everyone together and communicate his or her achievements. Under no circumstances should they spread ill-will about their predecessor or talk about a poorly managed department or function.

> When the previous boss has created a strong collective view of what the ideal leader looks like, it's difficult for a new leader to match that image . . .
>
> (Mazoni and Barsoux 2009)

Another challenge is when the predecessor remains with the company; comparisons are made, memories are short, and loyalty continues. More challenging is moving into a new role when the predecessor remains and is now your boss. This is almost a no-win game. Henry's story below highlights the challenges and opportunities that can arise with this scenario.

Henry's Legacy

Kevin was moving up the ranks of a global conglomerate in upstate New York. When he was promoted to oversee the global supply chain, he brought in Henry from Buenos Aires to replace him as Director of Supply Chain and Procurement. For Henry this was a mixed blessing: though he didn't know Kevin personally, he knew him by reputation and was aware of the challenges he was now inheriting. In his mid-40s, Kevin had been with the company for 10 years. Starting out in logistics, he moved into supply-chain manufacturing and later into procurement. He knew every aspect of manufacturing, buying, and logistics, from contract disputes to mergers and acquisitions. He loved his job and the company.

A no-nonsense manager, Kevin was renowned for his boundless energy. He was always on a plane to somewhere: if a client had a problem in New York, Zurich, Tokyo or Rio, he was on his way the next day and was never slow to weave stories about his accomplishments into conversations with everyone. He took pride in saying how little sleep he needed. He would organize conference calls with global teams, opening with, "Good morning or good evening; hell, I don't know *what* time it is. I've been here since 4:30 this morning." Every call began with a not-so-subtle reference to Kevin's energy, sense of commitment and stamina. The classic workaholic, incredibly intense, his job was his life and he repeated this like a mantra over and over again.

When the financial crisis led to budget cuts, Kevin's medium-sized team shrank to just a few, and most didn't like to travel (at least, that's what Kevin said). The company rolled out a new, lean austerity program and everyone was told to watch expenses, headcount and travel. Business travel was scaled back and short day-trips became the norm. Kevin didn't follow these rules. He had been at the company long enough to know how to maneuver around budget constraints and, after all, he reasoned, he worked harder than anyone else. He did not spend frivolously—even staff lunches and holiday events were co-funded; everyone chipped in.

He was shrewd in maintaining visibility, keeping a small coterie of consultants in business to support his projects. Through this group, Kevin connected with influential executives and everyone said the same thing: "Kevin has boundless energy."

From a distance, Kevin appeared to add considerable value to the company; hence his rapid advancement. Up close was another matter, and his excessive style showed. Henry was now working for Kevin.

In this new role, Henry felt the weight of Kevin's all-encompassing personality and grand reach. Henry's strengths were very different and his focus was on people rather than process. In his first 30 days, he made a point of meeting with every member of the team. From these meetings he learned that Kevin was not well liked. He was viewed as a decent project manager but was considered miserable at team leadership—hiding information, delegating minor admin tasks, never involving the team in big projects and rarely allowing travel. Most were relieved when he moved on.

New to both the role and the country, Henry's challenges included having to deal with a predecessor who was both glorified and criticized and, to make matters worse, who was still around—and in a senior position. Yet Henry was able to succeed in his role by:

- Staying connected to the in-crowd
- Carving out his own space quickly—differentiating himself
- Having a solid power network in place
- Speaking loudly and frequently about the team's accomplishments
- Providing consistent visibility and opportunities for the team.

It is not just the role and influence of predecessors that have to be taken into consideration in managing transitions successfully: the followers—those who remain in place—also come into the equation. Both Fischer (2007) and Manzoni and Barsoux (2009) believe that this is an area which receives too little emphasis.

With followers, predecessors and legacy, think back to James and Arroba's notion of reading and carrying and determine what the followers are reading and carrying into this new leadership scenario.

Equipped with insight of both predecessor and team, the next step requires an in-depth understanding of the decision makers and core groups. After you have some perspective on the decision makers, build a map of the people you would like to meet and the information you would like from and about them—their roles; their priorities; their motivations; their aspirations—and how these might influence your role. Seek their advice on what constitutes success within the company and how it can be attained. You should glean where they stand politically and whether they are potential advocates or adversaries.

Asking such questions provides insight into the various stakeholder groups, decision makers, and power networks and how they are aligned. Listen carefully to what is being said and how it is said. It is easy to be caught off guard by Mr or Ms Nice, or a Savvy Politician and it is important for anyone entering a new company to view relationships for what they are rather than what we want them to be. Be open-minded but skeptical—trust but verify—as you go about the business of building key relationships, affiliations, alliances and links to core networks.

Inside every organization is a "core group" that makes decisions, defines the rules and supports the organization (Kleiner 2003). Acknowledging this group and how to be connected to it is important for your career. While such groups undoubtedly exist, Kleiner observes, talking about them is often "taboo." I have found this to be true in my seminars when I suggest to managers that it would be instructive and useful for them to map such groups within their own organizations. Their resistance to the suggestion is often based on the notion that this would be both manipulative and time-consuming. My response to this is that they do this as a matter of course in their sales activities: why not then apply the same method internally?

The fact remains that we need to change the perspective and negative connotations linked with power networks. Leveraging insights from multiple groups (specifically those in power) provides organizations with a unique competitive advantage—innovative thinking. Harnessing this to the company's advantage can only have a positive impact on the bottom line.

Mapping out the power attached to influence networks/core groups/in-crowds—is crucial to understanding how decisions are made.

In the classic hierarchical organization, power is reflected in many ways: size, location and décor of office; make and model of company car; allocated parking space; and so on. It's not difficult to ascertain the respective power status of a department located in a penthouse suite and another in the basement next to the garbage-collection area.

Frank's Story

Frank, Vice President of Distribution, had worked for a luxury-fashion brand in New York for over 10 years and was renowned for his skillful contract negotiation. Now, the company was shifting its manufacturing base to the Asia Pacific region and had recently relocated its Hong Kong regional office to Guangzhou. When the company asked Frank to move to Guangzhou to help with channel distribution and business development he was reluctant to go at first, but figured a move to Asia would benefit his career. As part of the change, the company had appointed a new regional MD. In his mid-fifties, Bill was the quintessential sales person: a gifted speaker,

(continued)

ambitious and perceived as a bit superficial. With his gelled grey hair pulled back into a ponytail, black suits, crisp white shirts, and ubiquitous dark sunglasses, he had already acquired a nickname among local staff—Lagerfeld.

Bill's appointment had come as something of a disappointment to Linda, the Vice President for Business Development, who had harbored hopes of being appointed to the role. Linda had more brand experience in luxury goods and stronger connections within the fashion community but had nevertheless been passed over for Bill for reasons that at best sounded vague. She had great connections with the fashion group in New York and had an innate ability to negotiate extraordinary terms with all the suppliers. Despite her shrewd business skills, the speculation was that she was considered sometimes to be too emotional or too focused on the deal.

Originally from Hong Kong, Linda was a Princeton graduate in her late 30s. She had an eye for fashion, and was always impeccably dressed in vintage Chanel and handmade soft leather, Italian heels. She had been with the company for years and enjoyed the job, though from time to time she found the superficiality of some of the fashion executives hard to bear. When Frank arrived on the scene, therefore, she found his open, direct manner a breath of fresh air.

Earlier in his career, Frank had spent a number of years working for top agents in the entertainment industry and had a taste for the high life. He enjoyed travelling, relished the airline points, and the attention from all the service providers, but preferred dinners in Milan or Paris to lunches in Guangzhou or factory visits in Korea, Bangladesh and Sri Lanka. But he saw a stint in Guangzhou as a way to advance his career and see more of the world. Now in his late 30s, he worked hard to maintain his athletic build and perfectly groomed appearance. On arriving in his new role, he took the trouble to learn a few phrases in Chinese, with which to impress the office staff. He made a point too of listening to their concerns, though without necessarily having any intention to follow up on them. He had the happy knack of saying what his audience (whoever it may be) wanted to hear. The more savvy among the staff quickly pegged him as a self-obsessed politician, and were not impressed by his claims that he was not ambitious and had achieved his success purely through serendipitous moments or chance meetings. The majority, however, were persuaded that he was a nice, charming guy and they took his laughing declaration that "My only goal is to become Senior Vice President before I'm 40" at face value. Linda was among those who laughed along with him.

Frank spent most of his time on planes shuttling back and forth to New York or Paris. To his disappointment, he was only allowed business-class travel while Bill and others on the team travelled first class—a fact that he mentioned frequently to the staff in his office. He had a gift for delivering witty, backhanded compliments, generally choosing as his targets those within the management team who were not well liked or who he knew were not well connected to the company's power networks. His seemingly amiable nature and humorous delivery played well to the majority of his audience but merely gave further fuel to those who were more suspicious of his motives.

Despite all his protestations that he was not ambitious, when he heard that a new global role was soon to be available at corporate headquarters, he called the CEO to put his name forward. He then called Linda to tell her he might be relocating back to New York. In the course of their conversation, he indicated that she should consider applying for Bill's position "when Bill moves on." The conversation left Linda confused, as she knew Bill still had two years left to run on his contract. Even more bewildering was the fact that Frank should encourage her, rather than put himself forward. But rather than give full rein to her suspicions as to his motives for this, she allowed herself to be flattered into believing that she had his support. It was only when she reflected on this many months later that the real reasons became obvious.

Though they were by no means close friends, Bill looked upon Frank as something of an ally and they often met for

(continued)

coffee before work. This was a relationship that seemed to work well for both of them, though Frank often joked privately with his New York contacts about Bill's self-obsession. When Bill heard about possible openings in New York, he naturally asked Frank for his impressions of what was going on.

Though the two were alike in their ambitions, Frank had the stronger connections in New York and used this to his advantage, taking every opportunity to undermine his colleague's credibility and to promote his own standing with the power brokers at corporate headquarters.

Within a few months, Frank was offered a global position to be based in New York or Paris, Bill was offered a role in New York and Linda was offered Bill's position.

The CEO expected Linda to move into the new role immediately. Though Linda was delighted, she insisted that details of the benefits package that came with the role be ironed out before the reorganization was announced. This delay in the announcement of his own promotion frustrated Frank and, at the CEO's private request, he took it upon himself to reinforce the message that she should take the role and the details could be sorted out later.

When he called Linda with an offer in the discussions, Frank's mind was already in New York. After half-listening to her concerns, his advice to her was to "Take the role; the money will come later."

Sensing his distraction with other matters and feeling that his comments were colored by other motivations, Linda thanked him for his advice but made it clear that she would not be taking it.

In his conversation with the CEO the following day, Frank reported that all his attempts to persuade Linda to accept the deal had been to no avail. He couldn't understand her obstinate attitude. He indicated that her team had expressed concerns about "her emotional state and leadership style," concerns he was persuaded to believe were well-founded.

Frank knew how to time his comments for maximum effect. The negotiations continued but relationships were frayed.

> When her discussions with the CEO finally stalled altogether, Linda tendered her resignation.
>
> Soon after Frank moved to New York, Bill resigned, finding his position in corporate headquarters untenable as a consequence of Frank's maneuverings.

We're often taught to give people the benefit of the doubt, not to categorize people before we know for certain what they are really like. Think about the limited leadership transition period and use the same questions when someone new joins the team. Linda completely misdiagnosed Frank's ambitions and motivations, and more importantly wasn't aware of his contacts or his self-serving lobbying behind the scenes. It is easy to be caught off guard by the aloof, smiling personality of a narcissist. How many of us consider these complex workplace relationships, the large egos of the overly ambitious at play? Recognize that not everyone is an ally or advocate, despite first impressions, as Linda found to her cost with Frank.

What should we do when confronted with a narcissistic leader or colleague? The answer is simple: examine motivation and needs. Frank's motivation, for example, was to advance his career, move back to New York and be next to the power base. His goals were obvious enough but his methods of achieving them were difficult to detect.

> No one has yet devised the perfect questionnaire to diagnose what's commonly known as narcissism. But it hardly matters. Most people can smell it from across the company cafeteria . . . it's a familiar scent.
>
> (Carey 2010)

This whole situation revolves around motivation and organizational need. Linda needed to assess both the CEO's and Frank's motivation, and ascertain where the organization was headed. The CEO wanted to move the business forward in the region, a task which the CEO thought was beyond Bill's capabilities.

Frank's stint in Asia would help him move up the corporate ladder, and he wanted to move back to the power base in New York. Understanding Frank's motivation and role in this process is a critical piece of the puzzle. Frank is the conduit; he was sent to Asia by the CEO as part of a move to drive change. Linda needed to take a step back to evaluate the bigger picture and motivations behind this change. Having a clear map of the decision makers, business conditions and motivations of the executive team could have helped her negotiate the role with the package she wanted. Like Frank, she was an expert negotiator but failed to grasp the underlying drivers of change. She trusted but failed to verify.

ENDNOTES

1. Hay Group (1999). Emotional Competence Inventory (ECI) Feedback Report.
2. See, for example, Bridges (1997); Watkins (2003); and Fischer (2007).

CHAPTER 5

Mapping Power: Who's In and Who's Out

Vanessa's Story

Vanessa was the Senior Vice President for a global hi-tech company based in Shanghai, having joined the company after graduating with an MBA from one of the top-rated business schools in California. While in school, she had worked part-time as a marketing representative for the company and knew then she wanted to work for them. Originally from Singapore, she had moved to Canada with her family at a young age and spoke English, Chinese and Bahasa Malaysia fluently. She was also a gifted track and field athlete and had won numerous championships at university, where she had majored in business, minored in economics and had a natural proclivity for product marketing.

Vanessa started her company career in manufacturing and worked her way to the top of the business, in one of its fastest-growing divisions. With an eye for detail, she could

(continued)

recall stock numbers and prices of products sitting at the factories and warehouses across Asia.

Selected early on as a high-potential manager, she was promoted every two years and worked across every division and function in the organization. Understanding the numbers and having an acute sense of the markets, she had proved herself every step of the way. She saw potential in products that others thought would fail and was proved right every time.

Vanessa's strengths were her detailed execution, financial acumen and market knowledge. When she started something, she never let go and rarely failed. But her persistence in pursuing what she thought to be right sometimes bordered on the annoying for others.

Although driven, there was a humble quality to Vanessa's leadership style. She was constantly being given more responsibility, though she had never asked for a promotion. Given her track record at the company, she always believed her bosses looked out for her, even when, by chance, she found out that she was the lowest-paid executive at the firm. While this troubled her, she said nothing, believing that the company knew best.

Now, after 16 years, she was taking over one of the company's biggest divisions, with responsibility for a product that was the firm's largest revenue-earner.

Her boss, Andrew, who had known her for many years, felt that in her new role she needed to shift her leadership style to connect more with the broader organization and the community. He spent time with her sharing his insights on how the organization worked at this level. She had had other mentors but believed loyalty to her boss was more important than reaching out to others. This strategy had worked to her advantage and for more than a dozen years now had relied solely on him for building her career. In the interim, she had had only fleeting contact with her mentors.

Vanessa was the youngest person in the company to reach such a senior position and was completely unaware of how much others resented her promotion. Up until now she had been shielded from the rougher political waters of the organization and reached her level of success through hard work and determination rather than political savvy. Knowing that there were both team members and management disgruntled with Vanessa's promotion, Andrew advised that she should now give more attention to building relationships directly with her peers rather than relying on him for feedback on how she was performing on the political side of organizational life.

Though Andrew pushed Vanessa to shift her focus beyond the day-to-day running of the business, his counsel fell on deaf ears. Her usual counter was that she didn't have time for politics or for flying around the world building relationships and networks. She promised, though, that "Once this business gets going, I will take the time to make the connections." But the time never seemed to be right and Andrew eventually called in an executive coach to help her. Somewhat reluctantly, Vanessa went along with the arrangement and told her coach that a Myers-Briggs assessment the previous year had shown her to be an introvert who had learned to act and behave like an extrovert. "I was relieved to hear this," she confided. "It was the first time ever I had been labeled correctly for what I am. When you mention networking, self-promotion, speaking out at a large event, or attending a breakfast event outside of work, I freeze. If I go to an event, I feel completely overwhelmed." She conceded, though, that she recognized that this was a challenge she needed to learn how to overcome.

For the first year, nothing much changed. At the start of her second year in the role, however, with her new team in place and feeling more in control, Vanessa began to re-engage with her coach to uncover and develop the influential networks operating inside the company.

Meanwhile, market conditions in Asia had started to change, and the company found itself under increasing pressure from lower-cost products entering the markets. In responding to this challenge, Andrew made quick, decisive moves which,

(continued)

unfortunately, served only to accelerate the decline in the business, prompting Andrew to take early retirement. This brought Vanessa's position under the spotlight and, without Andrew's protection, she was suddenly more vulnerable to the prevailing political tides.

There were those in corporate headquarters who felt that Vanessa had been promoted beyond her capabilities. While it was widely acknowledged that she was a solid performer, there had always been doubts about her leadership capabilities. Now, with the business in decline and Andrew no longer around, she became the focus of discontent, both at headquarters and within the region. The mutterings among her own staff about her leadership style and the demands she was making on their evenings and weekends became louder.

Too busy to be aware of what was happening around her, Vanessa was largely oblivious to the discontent and the animosity being directed at her. In a very short time, the tide changed dramatically and she became the scapegoat for everything that had gone wrong. Guilty by association, she was seen as Andrew's acolyte, unwilling or incapable of moving away from a failing strategy. By the time she began to appreciate what was happening, it was too late. After 16 years with the company, this high-potential talent with a stellar track record was asked to leave.

When you reach the level of management that Vanessa had achieved, it's hard to go un-noticed. You're always on stage and someone always has a comment, but rarely will you be provided with feedback. On your way up the organization people stop telling you what's being said about you, and sometimes those same people add comments—positive and negative—to the water-cooler discussion about you. The strengths that helped Vanessa reach this level were not the ones needed for her to sustain her success. Many managers are woefully unprepared for the kind of transition that Vanessa was

Strong personal networks don't just happen at the water cooler. They have to be carefully constructed.

(Uzzi and Dunlap 2005)

asked to make. Many managers I work with have the same feelings as Vanessa and rarely take time to manage perceptions. Not many people like to engage nor want to find out what is being said about them—but it is critical.

There are a number of things that she could and should have done to secure her position:

- **Build a network early**: When things started to unravel, Vanessa had no-one to tap into. It was too late in her career to start thinking about networks. When the organization changed, many of her connections left the company. Vanessa clung to patterns of behavior that had served her well previously: she had never put much stock in the value in networks and did not appreciate the impact of not being connected to core groups of power until it was too late.[1]

- **Manage perceptions:** Vanessa's reputation preceded her. She was viewed as a detailed task master lacking strategic thinking, even after Andrew provided her with feedback and a coach to help her understand how to network across the organization. When the going got tough, she reverted to type, believing that putting her nose to the grindstone and staying focused were the keys to success. Vanessa was viewed as smart, but not tactical; many believed that she was simply a cipher for Andrew's views, someone without an opinion or an original thought of her own. For her part, Vanessa thought spending time on managing her reputation was ridiculous and seemed content to let her previous successes speak for themselves. What she failed to realize was that the higher she

In today's networked society, employees can manage personal networks, rather than rely on outdated, ever-changing organizational charts.

(Nardi, Whittaker and Schwarz 2000)

rose in the organization, the greater the need for networking and for managing her reputation.

As we have seen throughout this book, power and perception matter. When we talk about power and leadership, often negative stereotypes emerge—leaders using their position to coerce others into doing their bidding. This is what Keltner (2007–08) refers to as "the paradox of power"—the need to understand the negative side of power to appreciate its positive side. He suggests that there is a need to embrace the negative and positive sides of power simultaneously to appreciate the importance of promoting "a more socially-intelligent model of power." A critical element of savvy is knowing where power lies inside your organization. Bearing in mind that power does not always sit in organizational charts, the following questions may provide a useful starting point for discovering where the real power in your organization is located:

- Who goes to lunch with whom?
- Who interrupts whom at meetings?
- Who controls or has access to key people and private information?
- Who controls resources (budgets, money, people)?

Morgan (1997) includes personal power among the important sources of power in organizations. When I talk about power in my workshops, many participants talk about "owning" their own power. This makes perfect sense, as power is the ability to control one's surroundings. A manager experiencing powerlessness feels trapped and not in control—hardly a feeling that anyone wants to own or live with for any length of time. Power begins with you—your ability to act, engage and be an active member of the organization (Kouzes and Posner 2002). But these same participants often tend to forget or disregard other forces of power operating across the organization: those with legitimized formal authority, or anyone controlling resources, access to decisions, knowledge and information. When we think of resources, we often think "money", but anyone who controls a budget has power. We also need to recognize specialized skills (creative animators in digital entertainment or coders in high-tech industries, for example). However, the crucial source of power inside organizations is informal power—people with connections, networks and alliances are the ones to watch and get to know. This informal power equates to influence, and knowing how to use this influence for the benefit of the project or the organization (Morgan 1997).

Some people are incredibly intuitive. They can walk into a room and instantly spot who has power and who doesn't—these are the people that speak to you while looking over your shoulder for someone more important.

Others work from a different frame of reference, believing (like Vanessa) that achieving a position of importance requires heads down and hard work. They believe that the way to get ahead is based on the technical skills and experience they bring to bear. This may seem like sound common sense, and it is—up to a point. However, as you ascend the corporate ladder, this understanding of the dynamics of organizations can become trapped in time, naive and too narrowly focused and can result in a failure to see the world for what it is. Such people are often unaware of the social dynamics operating around them, and even if they do manage to figure it out, they don't know how to change.

If you are not gifted with an intuitive sense, try an analytical approach. Draw a map of who has power and who doesn't; who's connected to whom and how it all links back to you, directly or indirectly; who has a stake in your success, and who may view you as an obstacle. See Figure 5.1. Think about your organization as a network and start building the links.

Social media such as Facebook, LinkedIn, Twitter, and other social-network sites reinforce the old adage, "It's not what you know, it's who you know." As Tobak (2010) points out, "ten thousand

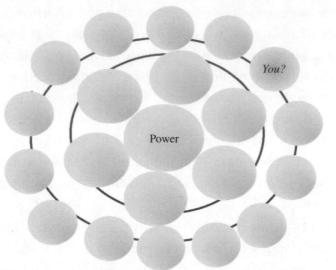

Figure 5.1   Power & Influence Map

facebook-and-twitter-fans aren't worth ten solid network relationships to an executive."

Think about the influence and power networks inside your company and ask: "Where am I?" If you're not connected to power, how
do you get connected?

When you first begin studying power, look at the hierarchy—
who's at the top and who holds the cash—bearing in mind that
power is not always synonymous with title. Power can be found
within informal networks and colleagues with influential links to
those in power.

How do you build on this map of power and influence networks?
Perhaps the best place to begin is with your location: are you inside
or outside of corporate headquarters? Employees working outside
corporate headquarters need to consider the role, impact and influence of corporate headquarters. Where are decisions made?

Considering the following points may help you to complete
your map:

1. List the names of decision makers.
2. Figure out how you are connected to this group.
3. Determine how your boss is connected to this group.
4. Consider how or if your team is connected to this group.
5. Assess how visible you and your team are to this group.
6. Observe how this decision-making group thinks.
7. Try to determine what is of critical importance to this group.
8. Plot where you are on this map.

Having such information brings you much closer to selling ideas to this group. Being connected to power and influence networks is one of the most important steps you can take to build political-awareness skills and your career.

Power and politics go hand in hand. You can't have one without the other and understanding the power dynamics at work inside your organization is the first step to becoming savvy. Having identified where the power lies, you need to be prepared to interact and engage with all the influence networks so that you know who knows whom, how decisions are made and by whom, and who the naysayers, resisters or stonewallers are. Remember, this map should *not* resemble an organizational chart or be filled only with the names of senior executives. It should also include the informal power networks *within each department and functional area in the organization.*

> Not everybody is obsessed with power or money, but few people would refuse more of either if it were offered to them.
>
> (Dubrin 1990)

Once you take this step, the plan will unfold and you will begin to see links, connections and probably a few gaping holes. Your job is to plug the holes. One effective way of doing this is to invite people of influence to lunch and ask them for the secrets of their success. Most, if not all, executives enjoy talking about themselves and do not always have this luxury. Tell them what projects you're working on and ask for their insights and advice. You could even ask if they would consider being your mentor.

By establishing such connections, you are likely to find out if there's any resistance to those projects, and from whom. Map your adversaries and keep them close. Find out what's being said about you and your team and use your connections to manage perceptions. If the perception is wrong, then you need to work with this group to change it. A positive word-of-mouth campaign from an influential colleague pays dividends.

It is important that you start thinking this way early in your career, or when you take on a new role. While it may not be stated explicitly, it should be taken as a given that connecting with power is part of your role. Organizations spend an extraordinary amount of time and energy crafting job descriptions, but rarely do these documents spell out the real measurements for career success. Your job description *should* say, "Find the most influential person inside the company, take them to lunch and stay connected to them for the remainder of your career." What happens in most places, though, as Brandon and Seldman (2004) found, is that many managers are uncertain about what really matters and subsequently go through a tremendous guessing game about how to achieve success.

Another benefit to mapping and being connected to power is that even if you are uncomfortable talking about yourself you will have a team of people that will do this for you: your own PR agency right at your fingertips. Find the "connectors" inside your organization; those who know everyone, with broad and deep links across multiple functions, industries and geographies. Gladwell (2000) discusses what he calls the "Law of the Few," illustrating the vital role of a connector. The rise of social networks such as LinkedIn and Facebook provides visual evidence of these connectors, and their connections. If you are disinclined to build a power map of networks, find one or two connectors in your organization and build on the Law of the Few. Contrary to what many might think, this is not being manipulative: it's being shrewd.

Many people tell me they don't have time to attend the holiday party or feel uncomfortable at after-hours drinking events. However, not showing up at such things can be a career-limiting move. Show up, but have your story prepared in advance (we will look at this more closely in Chapter 7).

While you should view every encounter as an opportunity to tell your story, you should also be ready to engage others, encouraging them to tell their stories through questioning and, importantly, listening. As Simmons (2001) says, "sometimes the most influential story that needs to be told is not your story—it's theirs." Show up early and make connections. Here are three tips to consider in this regard:

• **Connect with intention:** Have your story down and have questions to ask. As you move up the corporate ladder, casual conversations tend to drop off significantly, which provides opportunities for you to engage influential contacts inside your organization in conversation. Have your questions ready and have something to share.

• **Connect equally**: Don't stick with the executive suite. Many great leaders that I have worked with have time for everyone and at all levels within the organization—from senior management to the receptionist, the security guard and new recruits. Everyone has a story to tell. Taking time to listen can often provide keen insights and opportunities for innovation.

• **Connect with fairweather colleagues**: Not everyone's your friend at work and the chances are that someone out there wants what you have or may think you're in the way of their next move. Sun Tzu's advice to "keep your friends close and your enemies closer" is worth remembering. Don't shy away from engaging in small talk with those who may resist or resent you.

Taking a delicate approach to politics and power does not help the neophyte manager. Knowing the networks and navigating power is a critical leadership skill that should be broadcast loudly inside all organizations. Not only does it help build careers, it also helps sell ideas.

Yet discussions on power or how to figure out power dynamics evoke the same uncomfortable feelings as talk of politics. Nevertheless, this type of analytical thinking has a role to play inside organizations and you should play a full part in this because not only does the generation of new ideas depend on it, so does your career.

When you know about power networks, stay connected and don't let time pass you by: the consequences of doing so can be both frustrating and damaging, as the following case study illustrates.

Marcella's Story

Marcella was an executive in logistics management. Originally from Spain, she studied at Beijing University and was fluent in Mandarin Chinese. On graduating, she was offered a position in Hong Kong working for a garment-manufacturing company. In this position, she worked across Asia Pacific and spent a few years in North America. Eventually she returned to Europe, where she was recruited by Klaus, a senior executive with a global logistics firm.

Klaus had seen Marcella in action at a conference in Europe and had been impressed by her knack for getting to the heart of the matter in difficult negotiations. Shortly after recruiting her, Klaus had moved up in the organization and had continued to do so and Marcella eventually lost track of him. Though she joined the company in the UK, she moved to Indonesia with the eventual aim of working in China, where she felt her language skills could be used to good effect. Though she was well-regarded within the company and worked on a number of major accounts, when it came to roles in China she never seemed to be in contention. Frustrated, she thought the best approach was to go back to school in her own time and arm herself with a Master's. The China market continued to expand but she was still passed over every time in favor of younger managers. When she inquired, she was told she didn't have enough sales experience.

Frustrated, Marcella thought about quitting and doing something completely different. To this end, she engaged a career coach and, in the course of reviewing her achievements, Klaus's name came up. He was now a very senior figure in the company and wielded significant power. If anyone could help her, he could. But it had been 10 years since she had last spoken to him and she resisted all of her coach's efforts to persuade her to pick up the phone and call Klaus. Her resistance stemmed from knowing the political landscape but not understanding how to engage or work within the power networks. She was worried about what others would think.

Instead of calling Klaus, she went to Human Resources but, apart from suggesting that she speak to her boss, HR had little to offer. When she approached her boss, she was told that he needed her in her current role; she would receive a raise and a bonus, but China was out of the question for the time being.

It was then that she started to entertain calls from executive-search firms. She also started building her network externally, speaking at logistics conferences, joining professional groups and getting her name out in the market. Unfortunately, she wasn't doing the same internally. She liked her boss and was reluctant to go around him to promote herself or her career. This only served to compound her growing sense of frustration and it was only then that she took her coach's advice to contact Klaus. Overcoming her doubts about what to say after so many years of silence, she decided to be direct and tell him that she needed his help. Her directness paid off: Klaus made a few calls and the organizational wheels were put in motion. Within a day, she received a call from the head of talent management to discuss career options. Things started to change. Although the organization was now looking out for Marcella, when she received a couple of very large offers with external firms, she took one that took her to China. Though her company pleaded with her to stay, it was too late: she had made up her mind.

The message here is simple: Don't wait too long. No-one wins.

ENDNOTE

1. Uzzi and Dunlap (2005) highlight the value of information and power brokers to sell ideas, drive innovation and create opportunities. They recommend constructing better networks by connecting with disparate groups. Such groups might be professional organizations or groups outside of work, in the community, on the soccer pitch, or in non-profit or charitable organizations.

CHAPTER 6

Managing Perceptions

If understanding power is the first step to being savvy, managing how you and your team are perceived by others is a critical next step and one of the hardest to tackle.

How many of us actually think about how we are perceived and how we can manage those perceptions? When I ask my workshop participants this question, few raise their hands. Yet, managing perceptions is a critical component of career management and leadership development. There's hardly a leader on the planet that doesn't know what's being said about him or her! Before asking your network what's being said about you, you need first to engage in a little self-examination on how you want to be perceived. Consider the following questions:

- Are you an active participant and visible at meetings?
- Are you considered someone with influence and power?
- Are you viewed as a thought partner or expert in your field?
- Does this perception match your career goals?

- Does your current network support your career aspirations?
- Are there any misperceptions about you floating around?

In our example in the previous chapter, Vanessa was lucky to have a boss who looked out for her and knew her blind spots. Once he moved on, however, Vanessa was left with a legacy to manage.

There are three questions that we all need to think about:

1. How do you manage perceptions for your career progression?
2. How do you change perceptions?
3. How do you let others know you're changing?

If you're hesitating about taking this step, a safe route is to start by asking your friends, family or close colleagues for their perceptions of you. Bear in mind, though, that friends tend to massage your ego, tell you everything you want to hear, and validate your strengths but rarely share your blind spots or point out your development needs.

As you work through your network, don't forget to include the naysayers: your adversaries may tell you more than you want to hear, but you need to have this information.

This process also requires that you read between the lines, listen for the meaning that is often hidden behind the words you hear. Consider the following statements, for example:

"George is a fantastic thinker in marketing research *but* not very strategic."

"Frank is very good with clients and his team, *but* he's a bit too nice."

"Nicky is amazingly strategic and detailed, *but* not quite a real team leader yet."

You'll notice that everything in the first half of these sentences is undercut by one simple word: "but." Anyone hearing this may draw the conclusion perhaps that George is too detailed, Frank can't make tough decisions, and Nicky is hard on people.

The good news is that if someone tells Kevin, Frank and Nicky what is being said about them, they can plan to do something to change those perceptions.

> The BUT problem . . . the danger that attends those who are regarded as being technically competent "but" who are seen as lacking social and political sensitivity.
>
> (Buchanan 2008)

There are traditional ways to find out what is being said about you, including performance reviews, 360 assessments,[1] and feedback from your boss. Start with these, but also find other ways to determine what's being said about you. These are the official avenues, but to find out what's being said about you *when you're not in the room* tap into other avenues and sources.

- **High-potential talent groups:** The high-potential talent group inside your company often has its collective ear to the ground, is skillful at managing the airwaves and knows who's on or off the talent charts. This makes them a good group to connect with and to find out what's being said about you. A senior HR professional told me he frequently glanced through his organization's high-potential group's connections on LinkedIn or Facebook to see who they were connected with. This, he believed, gave him a clearer insight into what these individuals were doing and thinking: who might be thinking of leaving, who was connected to whom, and whom he could connect for future recruitment. There, he was also able to read comments on difficult leaders to work with and for. The incessant chatter of seemingly inconsequential conversations provided a pipeline of rich data.
- **Executive-search consultants:** Executive-search firms know talent in the market—that's their job. Though they don't normally

talk openly about candidates, if you know an executive-search consultant in your industry that you trust, build a rapport and find out what's being said about you. Use this contact as another touch-point for information. You may be surprised to learn how much they know about you, although the replies may be more discreet than direct.

- **Mentors, advocates and sponsors:** Having a mentor, sponsor or advocate within the company is another angle to hear what's being said about you. Advocacy and sponsorship are becoming the buzzwords inside multinational organizations. Deutsche Bank, Cisco Systems, Citibank and IBM have all started advocacy or sponsorship programs to build and sustain a cultural- and gender-rich base of talent. Within Ernst & Young, this is called "Career Watch." The role of an advocate is to ensure everyone feels they are part of the organization. An advocate speaks up for you during talent meetings, promotions and appointments on key projects. Many organizations are finding that advocacy provides a globally diverse workforce with connections to influence networks inside organizations and engineers visibility at all levels for everyone.[2] A mentor can do much the same thing.

MANY A TRUE WORD. . .

Early in my career, I worked for a wickedly funny business leader, Carl. Carl had grown up in the tough neighborhoods of New York. He sold wines and spirits to the restaurants in New York and later in Las Vegas. He was a hard-driving, leathery veteran, incredibly insightful and with a gift of the gab. Carl always made jokes and you'd only hope these weren't about you; he was spot on about individual foibles. He had a great way of giving feedback on your blind spots through endless jabs at your character. The chances of finding a Carl inside organizations today are rare; these days, everyone is more cautious about what they say. Nevertheless, there's a lot to be said for the accuracy of the old proverb "Many a true word is spoken in jest."

When someone creates a laugh at your expense, don't necessarily write it off as a joke: listen and pay attention to what's going on behind the words. While it may just be a throwaway remark designed to lighten the atmosphere, this may have been prompted by something altogether more serious, with more sinister implications for your career, as the following story illustrates.

Shelly's Story

Shelly, the head of marketing for a pharmaceutical firm, had joined the organization right after college. Smart and savvy, she was always in a good mood and rarely had a negative comment about anyone.

The company had recently gone through a restructuring and planned to combine two marketing functions. Shelly was one of the candidates. The other was Irene. Like Shelly, Irene had a solid track record in event management, marketing and branding. She had been with the company slightly longer than Shelly and had a solid network in place. She had previously supported the Executive Vice President of Marketing on two global events and remained close to the team. Like Shelly, Irene had a bubbly personality and was viewed as something of a cheerleader.

Shelly and Irene were both ambitious but their approaches were markedly different. Where Shelly's meetings were planned to the minute and everyone left with an action plan, Irene's were a free-for-all, with lively discussions. Shelly was renowned for her punctuality. Irene was notoriously late for every meeting, particularly if Shelly called the meeting. Time and time again she would rush in with a Starbucks coffee cup and a ready-made excuse at hand: "Oh, I'm sorry I'm late. I just got off a call with Jim [the CEO] . . . I'll be with you in a second . . ."

Irene used lateness as a means of exercising power in subtly undermining Shelly, but her lateness became a problem, not only for Shelly but others in the function.

(continued)

Shelly dealt with this by playing on Irene's idiosyncrasies in a humorous way and took every opportunity to joke about her disorganization. As Irene rushed in, gushing apologies and excuses, Shelly would ham up the ensuing dialogue, mimicking Irene's breathless tones: "No worries, Doll, how long would you like us to wait?" This would inevitably draw laughter from around the room and from Irene herself, who would giggle, "Oh, Shell, I'm not that way . . . go ahead and get started. I'll be with you all in a minute . . ."

Sadly for Irene, the perception of her as the cheerleader took hold and moved into negative territory and labeling. Despite her marketing prowess, she began to be viewed as an airhead, disorganized, breathless, sloppy and always in a rush. Within a few weeks, Shelly landed the role. Not long after, Irene left the company to take up a role in another industry.

Montoya and Vandehey (2009) suggest conducting perception audit interviews, using the results of the interviews to cross-reference how you are perceived and how you need to be perceived. While they claim you don't need to do anything extraordinary to bridge the gap, I disagree. If the perception gap is miles apart from who you want to be, you need to put a plan in place, now! If you have aspirations to lead a department, function or business, you need to start acting like a leader today. Yet, too many managers wait, the gap widens and perception becomes reality, as the following story illustrates.

> What sets great leaders apart is their ability to manage perceptions. What people observe or assess as your ability to be a leader and your effectiveness becomes their perception, which in turn becomes reality. Perceptions that are not managed become rumors, then gossip, then backbiting, which leads to destruction.
>
> (Russell 2001)

Jerry's Story

For eight years, Jerry was a superstar salesperson in a small consultancy. He was viewed as a hunter – execution-oriented, smart and principled. He'd started his professional career as a lawyer for a large MNC but had made the switch a few years into his career and never looked back. He loved consulting, enjoyed the organization and excelled at the role. Bringing in more clients than other consultants, he had quickly moved up the ranks, and became the youngest partner in the firm. He was great with clients and a stickler for detail. He set the bar high and did not tolerate clumsy, simple mistakes. He openly chastised his team for delivering a botched report and was merciless if he saw a spelling error. To ensure the level of professionalism to his clients, he reviewed every email and proposal that was sent out. As the business grew, so did Jerry's workload. He was viewed as a perfectionist, bookish, controlling and results-driven. Nevertheless, his overly controlling manner was generally tolerated because of his ability to bring in affluent and influential clients.

However, when two new partners, Alice and Mark, joined the firm, Jerry's quirkiness began to be questioned more. Alice had an affable character, enjoyed building relationships and was not particularly attentive to detail. At partner meetings, it was clear from Alice's comments – though she laughed as she made them – that she didn't like Jerry's way of doing things. She'd say things like, "Give the energy account to Jerry; they're always looking for analysis and we know he's the king of the spreadsheet." And these would be backed up by equally cutting comments from Mark: "But don't let him near the Marketing VP, he'll kill their creativity because it doesn't come in Excel." Everyone would laugh and everyone noticed the changing tide: Jerry was coming to be seen as a liability and Alice was slowly gaining influence with, and the support

(continued)

of, the senior partners. She could walk into any room and sniff out power. She used Mark as her eyes and ears on the ground and as the group shifted away from Jerry, her comments, both inside and outside the firm, increased.

Alice and Mark were viewed as the young dynamos of the firm. Both were aggressive go-getters with upbeat, positive personalities and were always joking. Jerry, on the other hand, had a reputation for being prickly and pedantic. For the past few months, he'd had an unusually high turnover of subordinates. Despite this, when the firm wanted to move aggressively into new markets, as the best hunter, Jerry was asked to take on a new client base and build the firm's profile in a new industry. He knew the industry well but also knew that this would pull him outside of his key clients and far away from the limelight. Nevertheless, he viewed this as a positive sign that the partners had faith in him, just as he did the partners' suggestion following performance reviews that he required coaching to polish his leadership presence.

Alice began to move into what was traditionally Jerry's territory, and called on one of his clients without informing him first. When Jerry found out and voiced concern that this sent the wrong message to the marketplace, Alice apologized to the senior partners and to him, saying that she hadn't meant to trespass on his territory and had simply forgotten to tell him about the meeting, which was, she said, informal and arranged purely as a result of an accidental meeting with the client, whom she had known socially for some time. Reluctantly, Jerry accepted the apology and the Senior Partner's assurances that he was over-reacting.

The following week, Alice commissioned a cross-industry research study for which she had managed to secure a sizeable budget by going directly to the CEO. The project would not only have an impact on Jerry's clients but would catapult Alice to greater prominence within the firm.

The research project was not on the agenda at the next partner's meeting, however, and Jerry's boss recommended that he not raise the issue because it was still in its early stages of development. The apparent secrecy with which the project was shrouded was, to Jerry's thinking, quite out of keeping with the partners' usual transparent and collaborative approach.

At the meeting, it was Alice who raised the subject. With an indirect but obvious reference to the number of analysts and project managers who had recently left Jerry's area, she said that this problem would have to be addressed in light of the new project.

Alice had dangled the bait and Jerry duly obliged her by taking it, questioning loudly Alice and Mark's right to lead the multimillion-dollar project. Sensing the discomfort of the others in the room, Alice remained composed as she explained how "the client wants insights on networked communities, online groups and how these impact revenue. Your insights are important but, knowing your penchant for details, we knew we didn't have enough to give you. Right, Mark?"

Mark reinforced Jerry's unease with a reminder that "yet another analyst" had resigned that morning and a barbed comment about attention to detail.

The words hit their mark and lingered, yet not enough for Jerry to do anything serious about it. Needless to say, in the end it was made clear, even to him, that his days with the company were coming to an end and he left before the inevitable occurred.

Though it had been made very clear to Jerry what others in the firm thought of him, he seemed incapable of adapting to the changing circumstances around him. Despite the coaching and advice he'd received, he couldn't seem to break away from the patterns of behavior that had served him well up to a point but that were now working against him.

Jerry's colleagues had certain expectations of him, and this episode merely served to reinforce their view of him. Where he needed to thwart those expectations, he lived down to them. He should have remained calm and sought more information about the project. Had he done so, this might have gone some way towards changing his colleagues' perceptions, persuading them that he was taking steps to move away from his old habits. Instead, though, he reverted to type and, in the process, cemented the damaging view they had of him as a humorless pedant.

By the time that Jerry had accepted the need to change, and was taking steps to address his perceived failings, it was too late and proved too hard a task. But there's a lesson here that we would all do well to heed to ensure that we avoid finding ourselves in similar circumstances. By adopting the methods outlined earlier, you will know how you are perceived; what you need to keep, change, or let go; how to effect the necessary changes; and who should know what you're doing to change.

A 12-step program for changing perceptions and building your reputation

1. Find a mentor, sponsor, advocate or coach and tap into your power network.
2. Determine what you want to be known for and develop a game plan for achieving it.
3. Find out what your enemies are saying about you.
4. Remember the adage "many a true word"; listen for the "buts" and the meaning behind the words.
5. Talk openly (with those you trust) about your development.
6. Ask for regular feedback.
7. Do something completely out of character—if you're viewed as quiet, speak up at meetings. If you're known to be tough on subordinates, take more of an interest in their wellbeing and thank them publicly for their work.

8. Change your rituals. If you're often late–and known for it–come in early. The opposite applies equally.
9. Use humor as a means of making a point subtly/overcoming resistance.
10. Connect with your internal communications team or hire a PR firm.
11. Embark on a word-of-mouth campaign to promote yourself and your team.
12. Thank your supporters and sponsors.

If you have a strong relationship within powerful networks, lobby them to help manage perceptions about you. Once you have mapped your power network, determine how you are connected with this group. Perception management and power networks are inextricably linked. If you have a strong lineup of power brokers, affiliations and connections, use them to help perception management. Refine your image and, in the process, you can redefine your "brand," as we will see in the next chapter.

ENDNOTES

1. These are reviews in which everyone who works with you is asked to give feedback on your performance. They are more or less standard procedure within organizations today.
2. Advocacy or sponsorships started because multinational organizations wanted to ensure that talented managers outside the corporate headquarters were known, talked about and given visibility in a way that other programs—mentoring, coaching and the like—could not necessarily provide. Cisco and Citibank, for example, bring together their top 10 percent of talent to one central location for everyone to meet and then pair these talented managers with an executive advocate or sponsor. Citibank started an advocacy program specifically for women in an effort to break the glass ceiling and provide exposure to talented leaders from outside the corporate headquarters in New York.

CHAPTER 7

Reputation and Brand Management: What's Your Story?

For those who think it takes too much time to build a reputation, think again. It doesn't, but it takes only seconds to destroy it. As part of managing people's perceptions of you, you need to keep a close eye on your image and reputation—or what you might call your "brand."

Reputation is critical. If you doubt this, think about the staggering amounts of money that the likes of Coke, Disney or Intel invest in brand management. Just as these brands need to be managed, protected and promoted, so too does your personal brand.

> Reputation is the cornerstone of power—guard it with your life.
>
> (Greene 2000)

But what is your brand? It's your story, a promise, a purpose, and a perceived quality. Brands are powerful, intangible assets, and provide a competitive advantage to organizations *and* individuals. While organizations spend millions on brand management, very few people even think about their brand let alone spend enough time managing their equity in it.

A brand is a personality, a symbol of what you are and what you stand for. Branding began as a response to the proliferation of products entering the market and the need to differentiate between them. Brands provided clarity, differentiation and uniqueness. They are often described as having human characteristics: personality, experience, feelings, emotions and psychological conditions. As Brown, Ettison and Hyer (2011) put it: "A brand is a unique value proposition expressed in a relevant and differentiated way such that it creates preference and loyalty among a key audience."

How about you? What is your value proposition? Have you thought about how you're managing your brand? If you don't think this is important, the following case studies may help change your mind.

Casey's Story

Casey was an upbeat marketing executive working for a gaming company. Having grown up on a ranch in Northern Texas, she knew how to shoot and fish and how to celebrate success. She was quick-witted and had a biting sense of humor. She was very gregarious and spent a lot of time with the sales team, both during work time and after hours. Marketing was responsible for all sales events and Casey would single-handedly take it upon herself to organize almost all of them and was always looking for venues that would top the last event. While this was part of the marketing function, Casey was known as the party planner. The team liked to party hard and at their regular Friday get-togethers Casey was known to drink most of the others under the table.

When the heads of Sales and Marketing got together to discuss high-potential lists and development plans and Casey's name was brought up as a solid talent that deserved to be on the next program, some chuckled; others shook their heads as they recalled her Friday-night exploits. Though seen as a solid, valued contributor, Casey was dropped from the high-potential list. All the water-cooler comments and the boardroom talk had taken a toll on her reputation. The brilliant marketing executive with potential had been replaced in the corporate imagination by Casey the party animal—a moniker that diminished her and her career.

Carol's Story

Carol is regional Vice President for an Asia-Pacific software company with its corporate headquarters in Minnesota. She enjoys considerable respect in the company because of her solid track record and industry knowledge built on the many years she has spent in Asia. She is viewed as an expert in all aspects of software development and is well known in the industry as being exceptionally bright and a principled, though fierce, competitor.

Her expertise comes with an abrasive personality. She's intense, impatient and quick to make decisions. Her communication is candid and forthright, regardless of the audience. She is demanding of herself and others and everyone knows that if you present to Carol, you'd better be prepared.

Last month, her boss told her that she needed to work on her communication style: she had been too abrupt and dismissive, particularly with colleagues in the US and Europe. The comments he had picked up about her were, he said, far from flattering. Her response was to tell him that she didn't care what others were saying about her, and she didn't give it a second thought.

A couple weeks before the global strategy meeting was due to be held, two vice presidents from Corporate Strategy

(continued)

met with Carol to review emerging markets in Asia. Former investment bankers, the VPs had made frequent trips to Asia and were known to be lavish spenders, with a penchant for discussing business over bottles of wine at five-star restaurants. Carol had little time for them, seeing their trips as being more personal than professional, and a waste of time and money.

When, over dinner, they told Carol she needed to move quickly into Vietnam, Indonesia and India or lose significant advantage, this did not go down well with her. She had had far more experience in Asia than the two of them put together and considered that she knew her territory far better than they could ever hope to. In her usual forthright fashion, she was quick to let them know what she thought of their scheme and, in the process, pointed out an error in the calculations on which they'd based their business plan.

When they countered by telling her that she was out of touch with corporate thinking and long-terms goals, she told them in no uncertain terms that they had no idea what went on in that part of the world: "I live here. I *do* know how to work the systems here, and can tell you you're going at it the wrong way. That's that, gentlemen."

After some awkward small talk and a few weak smiles, the meeting broke up and nothing more was said about the strategy.

During the global strategy meeting, Carol's boss pulled her aside to discuss future positioning for Asia. He told her that everyone had the greatest admiration for her work, but he was clearly exasperated. Shaking his head slightly, he continued: "The general view here in headquarters is that you're arrogant, inflexible, not a team player and too conservative. This may well have an impact your overall ranking in the company . . ."

You can draw your own conclusions as to how this matter played out from there.

Though acknowledged as being exceptionally bright and principled, Carol is also known for her arrogance and for not being a team player. She has been made aware of this and thus has choices: she can continue down the same path or change the story and find ways to re-shape her brand.

The same applies to all of us. Once you've discovered what's being said, you can either reinforce the message or re-position your brand. The first step is determining your brand image, promise and value.

In this regard, Simmons (2001) sets out a number of stories that we need to tell about ourselves. The most crucial of these answer the questions "Who am I?" and "Why am I here?"

Organizations use a similar format when evaluating brand equity. The first question centers on identity—who you are; the second establishes meaning—what you offer. You need to consider your audience—what they feel or think about you—and what relationships you need to connect with to reinforce or change the message. Stories bring brands to life. Every leader needs to tell a great story, particularly if they want to maintain loyal followers, sell ideas or drive change.

Many organizations provide exposure for talented managers through meetings with executives. Such meetings provide a venue to raise the profile of a relatively unknown manager or give greater visibility to high-potential talent. Sometimes, though, they forget to prepare the new talent for such meetings. When this happens, the well-intended meeting can have the opposite impact.

I remember very clearly a manager at one of my workshops telling the following story.

"A few years ago I attended a global tech conference. The head of Human Resources spotted me as I walked into the dining room, and motioned to an empty seat nearby. When I sat down, she introduced me to the CEO. I was a bit taken aback and when the CEO said to me, 'What do you do?' all I could think of to say was, 'I work here.'"

In some organizations, this one line could limit a promising career. As we saw in earlier chapters, first impressions can be damaging and, as we know, perceptions last.

Of course, everyone in the seminar laughed, but this young manager was not alone in not knowing what to say in such circumstances. Workshop participants frequently ask me what they should say if they find themselves seated next to someone powerful at a dinner party.

You need to have your story ready and Simmons' book provides insights on how to prepare for such encounters—serendipitous or planned.

Stories provide others with an understanding of "what you want them to see about you" (Simmons 2001) and, depending on the way they're told, can make a lasting impression on the listener.

Develop your story and practice the delivery. One simple exercise on building your personal brand (told to me by the marketing manager for a large luxury brand) is to think of three adjectives that you believe describe you. Choose words that are memorable and have impact. Ask yourself what you can share about yourself that others might not know. Having found the words that fit who you are or want to be, practice them every day. You must be comfortable using these words, so that you don't stutter or stumble over them. Use them over and over again until they are part of your nature so that when you describe yourself to others using these words they know that you are being authentic.

The statements you make should open the door for more questions and ensure that the person to whom you're speaking remembers these words. Don't overwhelm people with information. Keep it simple. Once you have your story down, if possible work with a communications professional to build on the story. Ask your corporate communications team to help think through your self-promotion strategy. Ask your power network, mentors or advocate to spread the word.

Brands are not built in a day; it takes time. Once you have your messaging down you need to conduct market research—ask others what they know about you. Your mentor and power network can assist you in this endeavor. If this group articulates who you are and what you do, your campaign has worked. Storytelling and branding go hand in hand. Stories sustain your image over time.

PERSONAL BRANDING

Your personal brand begins with your "Who am I?" and "Why am I here?" stories. This may seem simple, but you will need to spend time reflecting on your values, aspirations and experiences. Reflection is a priceless commodity and an important aspect of leadership, but rarely do we find time to do so. Take time over the weekend or after work to consider these questions. Your personal brand unfolds from here. The information gained from your perception-management interviews discussed in the previous chapter will aid in developing your personal brand story.

In earlier chapters, we discussed the need for self-promotion, something that makes some feel uncomfortable. Building a personal brand counteracts this aversion to self-promotion. But remember that if you're managing people you will need to promote them too. Through very little self-promotion, having a recognizable, personal brand communicates your strengths, skills, and performance. Consider some advertising to build awareness. Your advertising comes from your network and other ties, casual relationships and acquaintances.

The notion of personal branding was brought into focus by Tom Peters (Peters 1997). At first, this was dismissed by many as just another marketing fad but there are now many more books on building a personal brand. These include Wilson and Blumenthal (2008), which provides a step-by-step plan in building your brand for success in business or careers. Other useful materials include Robin Roffer's Personal Branding Strategies (http://bigfishmarketing.com). Such is the importance of this topic that it is now seen by many as being much more significant than corporate brands. Your personal brand should provide an authentic view of you—something individuals remember about you, an emotional connection or how you made them feel at the end of a talk or meeting. Therefore, thinking about your brand takes time to consider values, your standpoint, combined with what others say about you and what you want to say about you.

Using the many resources now available, you really need to sit down and take time to prepare a checklist of how you wish to be seen. A good place to start would be with the question "What makes me unique?" Imagine going for a final interview for a job you really want and that is the only question asked. How would you respond?

Once you have your personal brand down, secured and embedded in the recesses of your mind, the next step is to communicate it. There's no shortcut here. Practice and be comfortable with your pitch. Most brand books tell you to consider your target audience, but it might be interesting to use a counterintuitive approach. To prepare for your pitch, don't think about your target audience; you're not going to know who's getting on the elevator with you. Your pitch needs to reflect every aspect of you and here authenticity is key: who you are and what you stand for needs to come through in the first 60 seconds. A powerful brand provides a connection and elicits a feeling from others. This emotional connection based on authenticity makes for a trusted brand. Tag lines wear thin: use words that incite questions. Next time you're on an elevator with (fill in the blank) consider a few choice words: "I drive innovation." "I am the conscience for the company." "I am a turnaround specialist." Each one invites a question from your audience: "How?"

Besides practicing your pitch, an important element of your brand positioning is your online presence. Social networks continue to evolve—you need to stay on top of these and join a few. There are hundreds of marketers and bloggers to help you with this positioning.[1] How you position your presence online is important, as most managers shy away from self-promotion. If you decide to do this online you need to find a balance, bearing in mind that much of the criticism about social networking is the focus on self. The insights, tips and techniques on how to use social media to promote you and your team stress the need to be clear and straightforward in sharing something beneficial, which makes it easy for others to connect with you. But one word of caution here: as recent high-profile scandals have shown, an ill-considered tweet, errant comment or tagged photo can damage a brand and destroy a career, and you need to be fully aware of your brand, your values and what you stand for. Think before you post: content is king and the internet remains in perpetuity.

I'm always surprised at the relatively small number of participants in my workshops who use Twitter, LinkedIn or Facebook. Belonging to these groups provides a vehicle for positioning your brand, image and expert status publicly and quickly. Belonging to LinkedIn groups and posting comments helps you build your profile quickly and publicly: the multiplier effect and impact are phenomenally fast.

ENDNOTE

1. If you want to read more about building an online presence and managing your reputation, a good place to start would be with Brogan and Smith (2009). Brogan's websites (2010a and 2010b) also pull together a variety of insights from notable bloggers on a variety of work-related matters.

CHAPTER 8

The Spoken Word: Gender and Culture Issues

Maggie's Story

Maggie was a top-performing sales director for a consumer-products company and brought in millions of dollars in sales. She had been with the company for nearly 20 years and, with the support of a strong team, she was usually able to sell management on her strategies. She was not, however, everyone's idea of the typically aggressive, fast-talking sales director. In fact, she was almost introverted as sales professionals go.

A deep thinker, Maggie came from a small working-class Hong Kong family and had learned her impeccable English from Irish nuns. She'd achieved high marks in Math and English and had learned the value of teamwork through an active sporting life at school. At work, she was very focused on results and had built a solid, loyal sales team. After a successful run in Hong Kong, the company expanded into China and asked Maggie to join the Shanghai office, where she had been for more than

(continued)

eight years now. She was seen as a strong negotiator, a good presenter and a great team leader. While sales were weak in other parts of Asia, they continued to be strong in China. Given her success, Maggie was asked to join a newly formed strategic sales team. She was in charge of their largest territory, and viewed as a key component of the region's success.

When the company decided to broaden the exposure of its women managers as a means of rectifying a talent shortage within its ranks, it organized a series of meetings for their high-potential talent to think through the challenges and redefine its talent strategy. The meetings were to be held at corporate headquarters in London, which would provide networking opportunities and exposure to senior executives that would also build sponsors and advocates for Asian talent. Maggie was invited to take part and flew over to London.

While this group was working on the organizational challenges, unbeknownst to them they too were being observed from a talent perspective.

To ensure everyone was engaged and on track, the company had brought in a facilitator to moderate the breakout sessions. High powered, he spoke quickly and loudly, and peppered his talk with English slang. In the first breakout session, in which the team was asked to brainstorm new approaches for acquiring and retaining talent in Asia-Pacific and emerging markets, Maggie was partnered with three male Sales VPs and was asked to be the scribe for the group.

The men—from Germany, the US, and Australia—all spoke English with varying accents and fluency. They were animated and energized and the ideas were yelled out fast and furious. Maggie struggled to keep up as she jotted down the cascade of comments. With a puzzled look on her face, she'd listen, and then write phonetically, often with mistakes.

Walking past the group, the Senior Vice President of Sales saw Maggie at the flip-chart, looking somewhat bewildered and tired. He passed on this observation to the head of HR, who had also noted that Maggie had seemed unable to keep up

> with the brainstorming session. The seeds of doubt about her ability had taken root. Within the setting of that one breakout session, Maggie's talent ranking had dropped, diminishing her career prospects at the company.

Unfair as it may seem, on such flimsy grounds are decisions made on people's abilities and careers, and more often than we might like to believe.

Maggie, a native Cantonese speaker who was also fluent in Mandarin and English, was put in a very difficult position. Taking rapid-fire notes from people who spoke quickly, and in different styles of heavily accented English, is no easy task and one that the Senior Vice President of Sales (who, by the way, had never left the UK) clearly failed to understand as he made the 10-second synopsis that sealed Maggie's career.

But he is not alone in rushing to judgment in such circumstances. We've all seen similar scenarios. We forget travel times, meeting fatigue and language dynamics and are quick to judge who's with it and who's not, without stopping to think of the repercussions.

Working across multinational organizations, I often hear similar comments on talent, many of which come from North American managers who have little awareness of the well-documented differences in the dynamics of language or culture that lead to different styles of communication.

The greatest cultural difference in intercultural communication is the degree of directness of speech acts.

(Earley, Ang and Tan 2006)

While in Western European and North American cultures communication tends to be forthright and direct, many Asian cultures tend to use indirect methods—a tendency shared by many women, too. According to Tannen (1990) and Trompenaars (1993), indirect communicators take more time getting to the point, with more emphasis on building a relationship and understanding the context of the situation. It is easy to see how such different communication styles can present challenges in the cut-and-thrust world of modern organizations. No amount of training in presentation skills will change thousands of years of culture or socialization. Yet how often do you see talented managers being overlooked for a promotion because their communication and presentation styles are different from the prevailing culture? I've watched many managers wilt in front of senior executives, and such innocent mistakes can quickly limit a career.

Randy's Story

Randy was Taiwanese, moved to the US for college and graduated from Stanford University with an MBA and a minor in finance. He worked in the entertainment industry for over six years before relocating to Paris for a new assignment as finance director with a global media company. Randy had a keen sense for numbers and worked closely with the television executives on ratings for the international markets.

Although Randy had a knack for numbers, he did not have the gift of the gab, nor was a good impromptu speaker. He had taught himself how to network and how to schmooze at meetings, but was never comfortable in social situations where he didn't know anyone or when he wasn't prepared. His real ability lay in being able to scour detailed charts and consumer statistics and turn these numbers into a story for the executives. Being new to the Paris office, he was invited to join the European regional meeting, which his boss believed would provide Randy with a good start in his new role and introduce him to many divisional leaders and power brokers within the industry. Randy prepared for the presentation with his usual diligence and was confident that he knew the European market well. At the meeting, however, when he was asked for some obscure information regarding Saturday timeslots in Poland, he was both surprised and dumbstruck. As he fumbled through his papers for an answer he knew wasn't there, an awkward silence settled over the room. No-one else knew the answer and nobody was prepared to come to his aid. When it became clear that an answer wasn't going to be forthcoming, the presentation moved on. Though the moment passed, the tension and Randy's embarrassment lingered. After the meeting, Randy was provided with a communications coach and instructed to undertake a course in presentation skills.

From an organizational standpoint, much more needs to be done to understand and embrace both gender and cultural differences. Women are not like men, nor should they aspire to be. Understanding the prevailing corporate culture is important. If the culture is direct, it attaches great value to succinct, precise, and direct messages. If indirect, conversations reveal only part of the message and silence plays a key role in meaning and context (Earley, Ang and Tan 2006).

While organizations need to shift thinking on what leadership looks like, individuals must modify their language and communication styles.

A global hi-tech company asked for my help to coach Bahn, a high-potential manager who had been selected to run one of the company's global functions in California. Bahn had been raised in Thailand before moving to the US. From his appearance and manner, it was immediately apparent that he was affable, intelligent and well-liked and I wondered just what his employers meant when they asked me to coach him on "executive presence," a term that is both widely used and very vague. Subsequent conversations with Bahn and his boss highlighted a few areas for development, most of which turned out to stem from cultural differences. After just one session working with Bahn, I noticed that he prefaced his questions and comments with phrases such as "I'm sorry, can I ask . . .?" or "Forgive me, but . . ." He did this at meetings, he said, because it would not be polite of him, as the youngest member of the team, to express himself without first apologizing.

In Bahn's case, "executive presence" was equated with language. Using tentative, almost apologetic words was not going to help his assignment in California, where he was expected to lead a team of experienced managers on a new software-development project. Bahn had all the technical skills but quickly came to the conclusion that using tentative, deferential language was not going to work in this context and would likely be interpreted as weakness. Both he and his employers learned from the experience: he needed to adopt a more direct approach. Unlike in Thai culture, it would not be seen as rudeness on his part; and they learned to take more account of cultural differences in their assessment and management of talented staff.

> In Thai and other Asian cultures, positive politeness and other politeness strategies are used when disagreeing with someone.
>
> (Phukanchana 2004)

Senior executives from North America should keep in mind that in some Asian and European cultures, using questions or starting off with an apology *is* the way to begin a dialogue, and should be aware of the dangers of making snap judgments on this basis. I once worked with a woman who ran a multimillion-dollar business. She would enter the room, sit far away from power, and preface her comments or questions with, "Uhm, maybe, could I ask something . . .?" She was petite, looked young for her age, and would sit back into a tall chair—which gave the appearance of shrinking—and immediately labeled by many as having little "executive presence." How wrong they were.

I recently gave a talk on women and language inside organizations. I presented a chart to highlight language differences across cultures and proceeded to talk specifically about women. One participant said, "I am French and we always say '*Excusez-moi*' before asking a question. Would this be considered weak?" Before I could reply, she stood up, raised her voice, and continued, "If so, why don't you tell US multinationals to change their culture?" If that is so, it was an interesting, albeit slightly naive, point. Admittedly, organizations need to rethink competency frameworks and talent-management systems to ensure these well-intended systems are not contributing to the problem in talent management. Many organizations have little awareness that such systems can hinder talent development. There is a clear opportunity to view talent as different, evaluating them on differences rather than simply comparing and rejecting on the basis of set rules and expectations.

Anyone who has worked outside of their home country for any length of time knows the differences in styles of communication can be challenging and sometimes frustrating.

Figure 8.1 below, is based on the work on cultural differences and similarities of Trompenaars (1993) and Fisher-Yoshida and

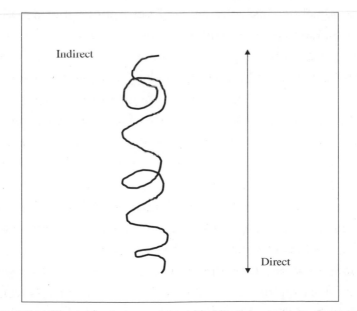

Figure 8.1 Chart depicting cultural differences and similarities of Trompenaars and Fisher-Yoshida & Geller.

Geller (2009), variations across cultures. The straight line represents cultures that value direct styles of communication; the wavy line represents "indirect" cultures. I use this chart in my workshops, asking participants to express their feelings, perceptions and assumptions when working across direct and indirect cultures. If they are from a "direct" culture, I ask how they feel working in an "indirect" culture and vice versa.

The responses are fairly consistent:

Direct about Indirect	Indirect about Direct
Not trustworthy	Arrogant
Evasive	Not credible
Beating around the bush	Emotional
Vague	Blunt
Ambiguous	Confrontational
Reticent	Insensitive

The adjectives, assumptions and perceptions fly! We all come to work with assumptions and perceptions, and need to be aware of these labels when making decisions on leadership and talent; no two people are the same. Leadership in the global marketplace comes in many shapes and styles. Indirect communicators typically think about the context, situation and the individual before they speak. This hesitancy or short pause before speaking can be perceived as weak, tentative and not trustworthy by others. When feedback is framed in stories, messages can be convoluted as the meaning becomes hidden. Direct communicators may misinterpret the message, become frustrated or believe they understand, when in reality they don't. In addition, direct communicators who speak without pausing or leave little time between comments can be perceived as aggressive and arrogant. This rapid-fire communication style results in hesitancy, reticence or silence. Appreciating the difference between indirect and direct communicators affects the way organizations evaluate leaders, talent, negotiations and collaboration.

Words are powerful tools for creating impressions, building perceptions, managing expectations and tipping the balance of success. The language of leadership is creating confidence: tentative language has few followers. Managers must move away from the tentative "I think, well maybe, uhmm . . ." to a firm "Based on my experience," or "In my opinion."

As we've seen from Maggie, Randy and Bahn, language is critical in leadership and in talent management. A small shift towards firm language makes a huge difference to your career prospects on a day-to-day basis. Using tentative language with an apologetic tone results in being labeled insecure, illogical, untrustworthy or incompetent.

Understandably, there are cultural differences in communication styles, some more deferential than others. First understand the context of the situation in which you work. If you're working with a US multinational, for example, and your goal is to move up the ladder, stay away from tentative words, even it requires you to write a script, use firm and definite language. Practice in front of a mirror before every meeting if you have to until it becomes more natural.

While communication is not the only competency of leadership, language and voice exude confidence and command attention. Whether giving a presentation, attending a meeting or participating in a conference, consider the following communication tips to increase your visibility and enhance your presence:

• The most obvious and overlooked point—be prepared. Even if you have given the same presentation on many occasions or know all the participants in a meeting, prepare. A new story or idea may pop into your head. This story takes on a new life, sheds new light into your work and enables you to be you. Storytelling is one of the oldest communication methods yet is rarely used at work. When you tell a story, the audience is engaged and your true self shows. It brings your authentic style into the room. Authenticity is the key to connecting and is critical in leadership. Practice, and tell a good and compelling story.

• Ditch the tentative talk. Think like your audience. Visualize a great leader: did Margaret Thatcher or Martin Luther King sound tentative? There are many useful sources of information on what makes a great presenter, storyteller or leader, Nancy Duarte's blog (www.duarte.com), analyzes presentations—every aspect and detail—and provides tips on what works and what doesn't.

• Go in to every meeting with a goal to leave having asked a question, summed up the dialogue, given thoughts or themes, or having made a statement.

• Stop, listen and reframe: every statement can be reframed. This allows time for you to reflect. Adopt a consultative approach, use firm words, employ reflective listening, and always ask a clarifying question or make an observation along the following lines: "Have we considered all the options?" (consultative); "Given what you said, it sounds like you want to focus on . . ." (reflective); "Based on what I have heard, I see a couple of" (firm); "Your idea sounds great; can you elaborate a little more on . . .?" (affirmative).

These expressions, reactions, and questions elicit comments from others in the room, adding to the dialogue and creating alternative solutions. Some people believe that those with power talk, but often the talk has little substance. Reflective listening or asking clarifying questions alerts people to your presence and adds to the body of knowledge, rather than dragging out the meeting with prattle. You remain positive and visible.

Shambaugh (2008) recommends not waiting for the right moment or the perfect words to voice an opinion: "We sometimes spend so much time crafting our message and thinking through the best way and time to talk about it that by the time we are ready and feel comfortable to speak, people have moved on." We've all done this—walking back to your office thinking, "I should have said this . . ." And, there's always someone in the office with the perfect question or insightful comment. Is this serendipitous or planned? As with comedy, timing is everything. But this does not happen spontaneously: preparation takes practice. Shambaugh's statement rings true for many of my clients, male and female. If you're uncomfortable speaking up, be prepared. Leave every meeting or presentation with a powerful question or give your participants something to think about. Pay attention and be visible.

But we cannot talk about communication without examining non-verbal communication. Every coach or facilitator in a presentation-skills workshop will tell you to pay attention to body language and non-verbal cues, 75 percent of communication is non-verbal. Even more it is challenging to interpret non-verbal cues across cultures. According to Earley, Ang and Tan (2006), "people with high CQ (cultural quotient) are very good observing others and mimicking their actions." Yet not everyone is equipped with a high cultural quotient. While there is value in reading body language to ascertain whether the speaker is telling the truth or veering towards deception, if you're working with cross-cultural groups, it's important to test your assumptions before acting.

There are six areas of non-verbal communication that may be displayed differently across cultures: distance, touching, body position, gestures, facial expressions and eye contact. Eye contact is one and trying to figure it out leaves many baffled. North America, more than a nanosecond of a glance may indicate friendship. In East Asia, prolonged glances may indicate defiance, disobedience or dissension. In other cultures, direct eye contact with women is avoided (Trompenaars 1993; Livermore 2010; Earley,

Ang and Tan 2006). Reading body language is not easy and it's best to test your assumptions before interpreting and reacting—as the following story highlights.

A finance manager in Hong Kong tells her boss, "You just can't trust the Japan team." "Why?" he asks. "They never give a straight answer: just talk round and round the subject," she says. "I think they are hiding something. I don't trust the revenue reports."

"You go through every spread sheet ensuring the numbers are valid, right?"

"Yes, of course," she replies.

"And are they correct"?

"Yes," she responds, completely missing the point.

Think about this situation: an entire culture has been tainted purely on the basis of differences in communication styles.

Communication studies across gender and culture have been around for a long time. Tannen (1990) focuses on the differences in conversational style between men and women. Interestingly, research has shown that what makes women different from men linguistically is what makes women great in cross-cultural leadership positions. Women look for common ground, connections and ways to relate. Men also communicate by staking their claim and taking a stand. These traits and communication patterns begin on the playground.

What are the conversational differences between men and women? Tannen (1990) and Buchanan and Badham (2008) observed the following differences in the concerns and approaches that inform the styles of communication favored by men and women:

Men	Women
Status	Connections
Power	Closeness
Independence	Intimacy
Win	Close
Avoid failure	Avoid isolation
Seek control	Seek understanding
Adversarial	Synergistic
Transmit information	Maintain interaction
Advice	Connections
Prefer inequality	Prefer equality

Observe women and men in the workforce on a day-to-day basis and you can't fail to note such differences. An appreciation of these linguistic and cross-cultural differences can be challenging and/or misleading. Working across the multiple cultures in the Asia Pacific region, many managers were wrongly labeled as weak or lacking in executive presence but the opposite is true. Women I've worked with include senior civil servants in Hong Kong and China, senior executives, philanthropists and filmmakers in Singapore, Vietnam, Japan and Korea. Though driven and clearly successful within their chosen fields, they remain self-effacing and "indirect" in presenting themselves to the world. Building an understanding of such differences helps productivity, builds tolerance and creates an open, candid environment. It is worth bearing in mind, though, that not all women or all Asian cultures behave in the same way. Always beware of the dangers of trading in stereotypes.

Women are *perceived* to be indirect in communication, but that does not mean that *all* women are indirect. What happens when women have a preference for direct communication styles? Labels

stick and negative comments buzz. While it is important to understand and appreciate differences, it is equally important to remember
that we are all unique. I was asked to coach a Korean executive
in "leadership presence." When I pressed for more detail, her boss
mentioned communication styles; she was viewed as being too
aggressive. During my coaching sessions, I did not experience this
"aggressive" style: she was smart, spoke her mind and did not suffer fools gladly, working for a consulting firm where such qualities
are generally valued. Looking deeper into the situation, I discovered
that it was not her communication style that was the problem but a
case of unconscious bias on the part of the partners in the firm. They
believed that she was someone who *should* have been quieter.

CHAPTER 9

The Politics of Performance Management

Performance appraisals are nerve-wracking for all concerned. But, many scholars and organizations argue, they also take up a great deal of time and energy that could be better directed elsewhere.

The alleged primary purpose of perform-ance reviews is to enlighten subordinates about what they should be doing better or differently. But I see the primary purpose quite differently. I see it as intimidation aimed at preserving the boss's authority and power advantage. Such intimidation is unnecessary, though: The boss has the power, with or without the performance review.

(Culbert 2008)

There are scores of books on how to give, receive, prepare and roll out performance-appraisal systems, though few discuss the political side of the process.

By their very nature, performance appraisals give one person power over another and the challenges this throws up are compounded when the reviews are conducted in an organization undergoing change, downsizing or a merger, when the general unpredictability of what may happen often makes it difficult for the reviewer to be objective. Politics permeates the appraisal process and has an impact on evaluations (Karppinen 2007) and, as Longenecker, Sims and Goia (1987) point out, "the formal appraisal process is indeed a political process, and few ratings are determined without some political consideration."

As we have seen, there is always a positive and negative side to organizational politics. The positive focuses on career advancement, selling ideas and recognizing success through strategic visibility or self-promotion. The negative appears when status is diminished or team members are pegged against one another to fit a bell curve, resulting in negativity towards the organization. In this, favoritism—simply liking or disliking someone—can play a crucial role, particularly in reviews.

Culbert and Rout (2010) talk candidly about the failures of these processes to judge performance and their conclusion that the performance-review process "destroys morale, kills team work and hurts the bottom line" sums up concisely what many practitioners believe.

One organization I consulted with demanded total compliance with performance appraisals. If anyone missed the mark, HR staff lost part of their bonus. Once a year, HR dropped everything and started the cycle of performance reviews. The team would spend hours communicating the importance of reviews, and providing training on *how to fill out forms* (not on how to give feedback or have a real conversation). It spent an extraordinary amount of time ensuring that everyone completed and signed the forms correctly.

If the general intent behind reviews is to drive performance, this company completely missed the mark. Relegating this task to the HR department to act as "enforcers" policing the function renders the process useless.

In many companies, performance reviews are undertaken simply for their own sake and serve no useful function. They are seen as a

The norm is a harrowing hour's conversation during which you are forced to swallow an indigestible mix of praise and criticism referring to long-ago events, which leaves you demotivated and confused on the most basic question: am I doing a good job? The resulting form is then put on file, making you feel vaguely paranoid, even though you know from experience how much attention will be subsequently paid to it: none whatsoever.

(Kellaway 2010)

chore, a mechanical process to be gone through and dispensed with as quickly as possible so that the various departments can get back to business. The problem is that all too often in such circumstances the results are used as the basis for determining promotions and merit increases.

The question of whether performance reviews and pay raises are related is a hotly contested issue. While most employees believe they are, Culbert disagrees, describing the "idea that pay is a function of performance, and that the words being spoken in a performance review will affect pay" as "bogus."

While some HR professionals believe linking compensation to performance may have a negative impact on morale and does not necessarily drive more performance, others believe that making the link provides the objective measure needed to determine increases. The original intent behind these reviews is connecting the employee's performance to company performance, which for many employees provides the psychological link between the annual performance review and pay increases. Pay-for-performance proponents believe this link provides the necessary conditions for the employee and the organization to reach goals and succeed.

Culbert believes that pay is subject to market conditions, which it is, but the boss determines the rating and the rating determines the percentage. The bottom line is that for a pay-for-performance management system to work, three key elements must be in place:

- Clear goals
- Timely feedback
- Rewards for good performers; measures for improving poor performers.

This is the point where performance reviewers fail. Culbert claims too few lines are spoken, the truth is often masked, and much of the dialogue has little to do with performance. And, if the review is positive, "the words spoken are likely to be more aimed at winning the subordinate's gratitude than giving a candidly accurate description."

Looking at both reviews and reward systems, something's inherently wrong with the system; either the implementation or the philosophy. According to the London School of Economics, the pay-for-performance programs inside organizations don't work: "Performance-related pay often does not encourage people to work harder and sometimes has the opposite effect."[1] During the financial crisis, when one Wall Street manager reportedly told his boss that he couldn't continue to report good news, because the numbers don't lie, his boss responded, "Make the numbers work: our performance reviews and bonus depend on it." True to Culbert's thinking, "the performance review is simply the place where the boss comes up with a story to justify the predetermined pay."

Irrespective of how thoroughly traditional appraisal systems are applied, many believe that they are inherently flawed. Few people, if any, are promoted on the basis of the forms alone, particularly when promotions are linked to who, rather than what, you know. The real issue lies with power, and the natural inclination to use power in order to influence outcomes or support self-interest. Some believe that political behavior is a normal part of the appraisal process, rationalized and justified for the good of the organization to "help balance effectiveness and survival."[2]

In his study of appraisal systems, Pfeffer (2010) found that "those who were able to create a favorable impression received higher ratings than did people who actually performed better but did not do as good a job in managing the impressions they made on others." People are becoming increasingly aware of the inequities built into performance-management systems and this has resulted in an increasing number of class-action suits being taken against organizations. Influential organizations such as Novartis, Goldman Sachs, HP, Lockheed Martin, and WalMart have been cited in cases alleging bias, systemic discrimination stemming from the subjectivity built in to well-intentioned systems.

In one such action (Carter vs. Hewlett Packard, May 2010) it was alleged that the employer targeted certain employees with an intense campaign of negative performance reviews, using highly subjective criteria that few employees outside of North America could possibly meet.

The payout and punitive damages involved in lawsuits such as these can be staggering, providing more fuel for those campaigning for these inadequate and anachronistic systems to be replaced with something that adds "real" value, measures "real" business results and ensures equal weighting for promotions, bonus and pay.

The bottom line is you can't remove power and politics out of the system. For some, getting ahead is all that matters and if the one in the driver's seat is behaving like Baddeley

> The idea that an executive might distort a performance review for political reasons is despicable.
>
> (Longenecker, Sims and Goia 1987)

and James's Fox, no new process will help. Performance evaluations are breeding grounds for politics and often the base of bias and falsehoods (Longenecker, Sims and Goia 1987).

An Ulterior Motive: Means and Ends

Gene had been VP of marketing for a consumer-products company in Singapore for three years and was anxious to relocate back to corporate headquarters in Ohio, a move that he believed would catapult his career to a higher level. To boost his claims, he had spent many hours on planes shuttling back and forth from Singapore to Ohio. His corporate connections were strong, and he'd heard that an opening in Global Marketing would become available in the next few months. Planning ahead, he thought it wise to have a possible successor in place and flew to Malaysia to sound out Serena, the only member of his team he thought capable of replacing him.

When he arrived, though, he was too late: Serena had just tendered her resignation and had already signed the employment contract with her new employer. She had, however, recently hired, Rajan, a new MBA graduate and she extoled his virtues to Gene.

When Gene's job in Singapore became available a few months later, Rajan was appointed to succeed him. The team was devastated. Not only was Rajan new to the organization, he had had no managerial experience to speak of and had never worked outside Kuala Lumpur. He was now managing an experienced, culturally diverse and geographically dispersed team. Within months, he was promoted to Director and within the year to Vice President, overseeing Asia Pacific.

Rajan was clearly at the right place and the right time. But how did this happen?

Gene knew the system well and had strong personal connections at corporate headquarters. He knew that his own aspirations would be strengthened by having a ready-made replacement for the post he was vacating. Being accurate was not as important as getting Rajan's promotion and rating pushed through. In Rajan's review, Gene wrote: "Rajan is a

> tremendous asset to the team; he stands head and shoulders above the rest in terms of customer focus."
>
> Although Rajan had been with the company only a short time, no-one questioned the validity of this assessment. A simple manipulation of the evaluation form was sufficient to land him a plum job for which he had few qualifications.

Culbert (2008) sees the performance review as "simply the place where the boss comes up with a story to justify the predetermined pay." For Rajan, the predetermined pay and subsequent promotion was completely fabricated to fulfill Gene's career agenda of moving back to headquarters.

Similar problems can also arise when a manager has too many direct reports to deal with in meeting the immediate demands of performance appraisal as well as their day-to-day responsibilities. In such circumstances, many resort to the technological solution to their problem— they simply cut and paste comments, irrespective of how well, or even whether, they know the individuals concerned. This approach may or may not be found out but, either way, it has a direct impact on the pay and career prospects of all those who are subjected to it.

We've all witnessed the bad side of reviews, and often it links back to overuse of power, hidden agendas and political favors. Many managers believe a good review is the way to get ahead, but performance alone does not guarantee a promotion. Performance reviews and the pay-for-performance schemes linked to them need to be re-thought. There are challenges from a cultural perspective and problems from a measurement perspective. And power politics plays a big role in all of this.

POWER, CONTROL AND PERFORMANCE REVIEWS

I once worked with Delia, the managing director of a consumer-products company in China. Originally from Sydney, Delia was casually dressed at all times, her Indian gauze shirts, flowing skirts or khaki pants giving the impression of a surfer or a hippie more than a high-powered businesswoman. Apart from a photograph showing her with the Dalai Lama and another of surfers riding the waves of Waimea Bay in Hawaii, her office was almost spartan in its decoration. Though she always appeared cool, calm and collected, there was a challenging directness to her demeanor. Being transparent was a guiding principle for Delia and she believed in being direct, open and candid about anything. Her goal was to build a work environment that operated according to the principles she espoused.

Despite her appearance and her seemingly alternative approach— her passion for surfing, yoga and personal transformation—Delia had always been both shrewd and ambitious when it came to managing her career. From the outset, she had made a point of surrounding herself with experts and consultants and, over the years, had built a close network of powerful and influential contacts. She knew the China market well, had a reasonable command of Mandarin and led with a firm hand. In short, she knew how to manage power well and stayed in close personal touch with those who wielded the most influence at the company's headquarters in New York.

Though the executive team found Delia to be a bit brash and a little too outspoken at times, they tolerated her idiosyncrasies because she was a solid sales person, known in media circles and within the industry, and she got things done. She believed in telling others what she thought and did not hold back, believing it best to confront others openly and directly.

She encouraged her staff to be open about their business and personal concerns, but had been known to use this information against them when it suited her purpose. For this reason, many did not trust her.

Delia wanted to use this same open style with performance reviews and called in an executive coach from Australia to facilitate dialogue sessions with her staff. These were to consist of compulsory communication circles, in which one person was required to sit in the middle while the rest provided "critical" feedback—saying something positive in the beginning but giving at least one crucial piece of feedback on an area in which there was room for improvement. At the end of the meetings, participants were asked to reflect on what they'd learned. The feedback, however, was not what Delia had been hoping for; the participants, eyes cast firmly downward, smiled demurely as they said that they thought the dialogue sessions were "helpful." Later, in private, though, they all expressed discomfort with the process, especially the part where they were each called on to provide candid feedback on Delia. Few, if any, had been willing to do so and little of any value came from the meetings. Some feared the consequences of being outspoken and all were ill-equipped to do so.

The whole exercise was a complete miscalculation on Delia's part. She believed that what had been shown to work in Australia or the United States could work anywhere. Completely disregarding the cultural sensitivities of her Chinese staff, she had attempted to impose a concept that was alien to them. They had gone along with it up to the point that politeness or fear would allow but, ultimately, the exercise had proved futile.

It has to be said that, even putting cultural differences aside, most managers would be reluctant to speak truth to power in such circumstances unless they were confident of having the support of their own power network.

Performance reviews and power plays

There are other ways in which performance reviews can be manipulated and used as power tools in the hands of unscrupulous operators. I remember very well a story told to me by Lucy, an experienced and successful sales director who was made redundant after 12 years with a company.

Market conditions had deteriorated and the company was obliged to make cuts. Lucy's position was one of these. Although she saw the downturn as being only temporary, she accepted the decision and continued to behave with great professionalism throughout her remaining three months in the job. In recognition of her track record, her long tenure and continued professionalism she was told that she would receive a generous redundancy package. The company even sounded her out as to her willingness to transfer to other regions, even though this would have been tantamount to a demotion. However, as the date for her departure from the company neared, she received details of the redundancy package which were inconsistent with what she had been promised. She asked a lawyer to look over the details of the package. When the HR department heard that she had consulted a lawyer, she was called in and told that certain unacceptable aspects of her performance (which they didn't specify) had recently come to light. Unless she accepted the package as it stood, they said, they would instigate a full performance review, on the basis of which they would be forced to sack her. The company had, to suit its own ends, misused its power to transform this from a redundancy into a performance-related matter. The choice was hers: she must take it or leave it. As it transpired, she eventually accepted the package, even though it was less than originally discussed. Interestingly enough, though, the HR person involved in this matter also left the company a few months later, ostensibly to "pursue other opportunities."

When I tell this story to HR professionals, they are generally appalled: in such circumstances there would be no need to conduct a performance review unless this had been specified in the termination agreement or it is for future reference or re-employment purposes. Often, employees who are made redundant are rehired as consultants or contract staff and organizations want to ensure documentation of performance is maintained. In other circumstances, companies may choose to use redundancies as a means of getting rid of non-performing staff, rather than having to go through the complex and time-consuming termination processes of issuing warnings.

What then is the best way to deal with problems that arise from a performance review?

1. Generally, the review process starts with the employee being asked to provide a self-assessment. Where this applies, you should write up a clear, factual account of your accomplishments and contributions to the firm. After your boss has conducted the review and you are shown the ratings, there is usually a space provided for you to comment and, if necessary, to disagree. Bear in mind, though, that your boss has the power to maintain ratings and comments and the company is not obliged to make changes in light of your comments.

2. If you think you have been treated unfairly by the review process, take the matter up with your boss, and if that goes nowhere be prepared to take it to the next level. In deciding whether to do this, you need to weigh the pros and cons, and ensure you have thought through the best alternative for this choice. Have a solid network in place or your complaint may not be well received.

3. If you work in a matrix or with multiple business leaders, you have multiple touch points and valid feedback partners to support your work and ultimately your review.

4. If client feedback is practiced in your organizations this is another source for your review.

5. Should you run into challenges, speak to HR. An addendum can be created and attached to the appraisal form and filed away for your personal file. If there's a gross misrepresentation that poses ethical issues or incorrect amounts, the human resource leader should escalate the grievance to the highest level required. If that fails, consult a legal expert, the ombudsperson or whatever other avenues there are in your organization for making formal complaints.

6. If none of these apply or are inappropriate, you may consider leaving the company.

As with many other instances encountered in this book, under-standing power and influence networks is critical to navigating these situations.

As you may have detected by now, I am not a fervent supporter of traditional performance-review systems, having seen how they can be manipulated and abused. If you believe that you have been wronged or have witnessed manipulation and abuse, there are, according to HR professionals, a number of avenues open to you to seek redress, depending on the particular circumstances.

If, for example, you believe that the person conducting a review has overstated the performance of their staff to ensure a bonus or promotion, what can you do? The responsibility for assessment lies squarely with the direct supervisor and/or leaders within the business unit, which makes it hard for HR to prove the allegations. Many organizations require peer calibration meetings as checks and balances to ensure that managers are held accountable for their ratings.

A way for organizations to ensure that managers cannot over-state the performance of their staff is to establish objective criteria on promotions—specific requirements, skills, job description, and development—and having others involved in the review process—a colleague, business partner or client. In some organizations, the man-ager's boss also needs to approve the promotion as another checkpoint. But as you move up the corporate ladder, there are fewer checkpoints or you may be too far removed from the immediate circumstances to know whether the promotion is deserved. In other words, if the manager makes a subjective case to promote someone, there is little you can do about it.

Most organizations have checks and balances in place with per-formance reviews. Some employ a forced distribution curve, in which a certain percentage at the top of their mathematical rankings are auto-matically promoted and a corresponding percentage at the bottom of the rankings are moved out. GE is one such company that uses this method. Another form of calibration is measuring performance against others in the same function, level, role or business—but this too is open to subjective judgments and political power plays. Some companies use promotion committees, others use a ranking system that involves input from multiple stakeholders. Some conduct audits in which corporate headquarters reviews the performance reviews to ensure that one group is not getting ahead at the expense of another and thus to ensure a balanced approach to promotions and pay.

Reviews or talent-management programs often tend to produce a very homogeneous group of people, who display the same characteristics as those who design and control the systems. The self-perpetuating nature of these systems is being called into question as organizations expand globally. Though organizations need to have representation from the communities they serve, many multinationals continue to suffer from what might be called the "people like us" syndrome, filling senior roles with the same type of people or bringing expatriates over to Asia to work in the regional offices. To counter these restrictive tendencies, Diversity and Inclusion programs began to be introduced under the aegis of the EEOC in the US 20 years ago. These programs are designed to ensure diversity—of culture, gender and the like—in the workplace.

ENDNOTES

1. "When performance-related pay backfires," London School of Economics, June 24, 2009. Available at: www.financialchannel.com
2. Karppinen (2007).

CHAPTER 10

Power, Politics and Sex

From prostitution scandals to corruption allegations to the steady drumbeat of charges against corporate executives and world-class athletes, it seems that the headlines are filled with the latest mis-step of someone in a position of power.

Lehrer 2010

This is a difficult subject to discuss but it is an ever-present problem and shows no signs of abating. There seems to be an unbreakable nexus between sex, politics and power and women often are on the receiving end of this unsavory side of organizational life. Let's be clear about this from the start: sexual harassment has less to do with sex than it does with exerting power, and control over others.

When I first started conducting workshops on political awareness in the workplace, sexual harassment was not a formal part of the curriculum until Lily, a young Harvard and Oxford-educated Chinese woman, told me of her experiences working for a US investment bank in Singapore.

Working as a trader, Lily was expected to go out drinking after hours with her (mostly) male colleagues. She didn't like to drink, but going out was part of the job. Her strategy was to show up late, put in an appearance, and leave early. By then, she said, her colleagues were often "too drunk to notice." One evening she received the unwanted physical attentions of one of the VPs. Lily politely moved his hand and walked away, but the flirtation continued.

The bank was planning a special event for select clients centered around the forthcoming Formula One race. Everyone would be in town and Lily was expected to attend what was certain to be what she called a "Cliquot-filled affair." Anxious to avoid any further encounters with the amorous VP, Lily asked me what she should do.

My advice to her—as it would be to anyone in similar circumstances—was to start with Human Resources. In my experience HR departments of US companies take such matters seriously and generally handle them with great discretion. She listened, but her reluctance to act was obvious. When pressed, Lily felt that if she reported the VP's behavior, everyone would know she was the source of the complaint and didn't want to jeopardize a career she loved.

I suggested she speak to the company's ombudsperson—every large organization has an ombudsperson, assigned to deal with harassment issues and ethical concerns—but it was clear she didn't trust this route either. While this reflected the state of mind of a young woman concerned about her career, it was a sad commentary on how two corporate functions that exist to help employees are viewed.

Since that conversation with Lily, participants in my workshops have been more than willing to discuss the sexual harassment they've confronted: sexually suggestive text messages and invitations from married senior executives; unwanted verbal and physical attentions; sexually explicit jokes. One participant told how a managing partner of a corporate law firm exposed himself to her in the office after hours. Another described a holiday party at which her 70-year-old boss asked her to dance and then proceeded to slide his hands under her clothing in front of the whole company. "I don't know what's worse," she said, "having someone make advances in private or being made to feel like the office slut in public."

These are not isolated incidents. Indeed, it is so prevalent in some countries and some organizations that harassment and sexual politics have to be dealt with as part of day-to-day work. Even when individuals are not targeted personally they are often obliged to work in an environment where such behavior is tolerated.

The US Equal Employment Opportunity Commission (EEOC)[1] indicates that sexual-harassment complaints in the United States have gradually decreased over the last decade. Whether this reflects a genuine improvement or that many incidents are never formally filed or go unreported, is not clear.

Despite what EEOC data might indicate, many new cases continue to emerge, even from such globally prominent organizations as Goldman Sachs, HP and Dell. In a recent case involving a prominent retail organization in Australia, the company's CEO was forced to resign amid threats of a multimillion-dollar lawsuit following allegations that he sexually harassed the company's publicist.[2] This highlights the necessity for organizations to take such complaints seriously if they do not want to put their reputation and brand positioning at risk.

However, in many organizations, a more typical response is to "just say no" and "forget about it, not worth it" or ignore things altogether and hope that things will get smoothed over. This latter course often involves a fresh round of power politics and psychological games.

Recently I met with a business leader from a well-known US global brand who had experienced psychological and sexual harassment from her boss. Somewhat reluctantly, she informed HR of what had happened and lodged a formal complaint.

The complaints procedure was supposed to be confidential but someone tipped off her boss and prompted him to adopt an entirely different approach to her. He soon visited her office more often and enquired on her wellbeing. He commented on how tired she looked, and suggested she take time off to relax. She easily saw through this feigned niceness as an attempt to discredit her claims, and ultimately decided it was easier to leave the company than press the matter further.

The fact that harassment is still a major problem, even within globally prominent organizations, is a clear indication that companies need to do more to monitor the processes in place more rigorously to ensure they fulfill the purpose for which they were set up. It is essential that anyone lodging a complaint does so without fear of reprisal or jeopardizing their career.

If anyone doubts the reality of the link between power, control and sex, or the damage this can do to individuals and organizations, the following story may well give them cause to think again.

Rochelle's Story

Rochelle, a recent graduate of Jackson State University in Alabama, had applied for the role of administration manager with a renowned logistics organization in Southern California. After a successful first interview with Leon, the division head with whom she would be working, she was invited back for a second interview, this time with Leon's boss, Justin, the VP of Global Logistics.

Anxious to make a good impression, she was slightly nervous as she approached Justin's office. As she was about to knock, the door flew open and she was greeted by an immaculately dressed, middle-aged man, who welcomed her with a flourish. Slightly unnerved by the gesture, it took her some time to register the fact that beneath the external calm of his questioning there was something odd and intimidating about the way he rocked back in his chair, tapping his fingers on his chest, or ran his hand over the top of his head but without ever touching his thick, gelled, locks.

After three or four fairly standard questions, out of the blue he'd said: "Don't worry; if you want the job, it's yours. These questions are only a formality. I only arranged this to make Leon sweat a bit."

During the brief conversation that followed, Justin made it very clear that *he* was the one doing the hiring and that *he*—not Leon—was Rochelle's boss. To emphasize his point, he told her that if she ever had an issue with Leon, she was to call him directly. Though shocked and somewhat confused by all this, Rochelle was relieved nevertheless: she needed the job and accepted the offer.

Any misgivings she may have felt as she arrived at the office for her first morning at work were dispelled when Leon presented her with a huge bouquet of flowers and a card that read, "Welcome to the team," and signed by Justin, Leon and a few of her other new colleagues. Warmed by this gesture, she was just settling at her desk when she received a call from Justin to ask if she had received the flowers. She assured him that she had and that they were beautiful. To her complete surprise, he then launched into a harangue about bad manners and poor upbringing. It transpired that he had expected her to pick up the phone and thank him immediately. She was mortified, and even more so when he then called everyone on the team and told each of them to remind her of the proper etiquette involved in receiving a gift.

As time went on, there were many more examples of Justin's demanding and erratic behavior—someone was always being publicly berated for a spelling error or for some other minor infraction of his ever-changing rules. There was even a report from the New York office of how Justin had demanded of a new hire that she stand up and "Repeat after me, 'I am stupid'." When she'd refused and walked away, he'd followed her down the hallway and continued with this rant until she'd left the office. While none of these other incidents had had any direct bearing on Rochelle, they had continued to unnerve her nonetheless.

(continued)

She was not so lucky at the annual holiday dinner, however, which was held at Justin's favorite Chinese restaurant in San Francisco. For some reason, Rochelle was seated away from her regular office colleagues and across the table from Justin and his wife, surrounded by wealthy clients and their wives. She couldn't understand why the seating had been arranged this way and felt completely out of her depth. Following her instincts and upbringing, she'd decided that the best way to deal with the situation was to be quiet, respectful, and speak only when spoken to.

As the evening wore on, she noticed that Justin was always looking at her and it occurred to her then that he had arranged the seating for just that purpose. Though he had never made any open advances, for the past few months he had been more than usually attentive to her welfare, with questions that strayed subtly into the area of her personal life. Once, when she had been away for the weekend, she had got home to find 18 increasingly drunken messages from him on her phone. He'd made no mention of those calls since and she'd decided that the best thing to do was to ignore them. In the meantime, she'd heard from HR that Justin had been speaking highly of her and her potential for a move into a corporate role. Being young and ambitious, she'd enjoyed hearing this.

The holiday dinner was to be the turning point, though. With his wife seated next to him, Justin began to be openly complimentary of her work, hinting that she was soon to take over Leon's role. Mostly, though, he'd complimented her on her appearance, addressing most of his comments to her chest. At the end of an already-bizarre evening, Justin and his wife had handed her an embossed Bible, with her name inscribed in gold on the front cover, and told her that they would pray that she would receive Jesus into her heart. They were beaming with joy when she left the restaurant with the Bible in her hand.

On the following Monday morning, she was confronted by an angry Leon with a list, provided by Justin, of everything she had done wrong that evening. She had apparently offended Mrs Justin by not speaking to her and had not been friendly enough to the other guests. (The one thing that he could not fault was the way that she had responded to the gift she had received. Over the weekend, she had selected an expensive card from a branded stationery store and crafted a handwritten note remarking on the beautiful gift and the lovely evening. She had had the card delivered to his home by courier.)

Rochelle continued working with Leon but the atmosphere was always tense. The childish and abusive games played by Leon and Justin continued, as they sought to outdo each other. Whenever she spoke about this unofficially with someone in human resources, she was told that, although he was known to be quirky and maybe psychologically unbalanced, Justin was well liked at corporate headquarters. As a relative newcomer, Rochelle felt that she would not have a leg to stand on if she chose to pursue the matter further and decided that her best course would be to leave the company and look for something new.

After she left, she'd heard that the company had been awarded a new contract by a large multinational, which had strict policies on harassment and took all complaints very seriously. Shortly afterwards, Justin was dismissed for sexual harassment and although Rochelle never heard the details of the particular incident, she did hear that it had released a torrent of stories about the years of sexual and psychological harassment.

Rochelle went on to establish a very successful career in Italy, working for a large apparel manufacturing company. Although scarred by working with two paranoid megalomaniacs, now, 20 years on, she feels, in her own words, "stronger for the experience." She is adamant, though, that "no-one should ever have to go through such treatment in a workplace."

Kim's Story

Kim, a first-generation Chinese American in her late 20s, had studied math on a scholarship at Stanford. After graduation, she'd worked for one of the top investment banks in New York, where she met Dieter, an investment banker with a flair for extravagance and a knack for timing the markets. A rebel at heart, he did not fit with established Wall Street firms and soon left to start a boutique investment firm in Hong Kong.

After eight years in New York, Kim received an invitation to join Dieter's firm in Hong Kong. While she had known Dieter only briefly, the talk she had heard in the interim about his reputation and bipolar personality didn't match with what she knew. She had grown tired of the culture of one-upmanship that permeated the banks and was prepared to ignore the gossip and take her chances in Hong Kong.

Once there, she found him to be a nice, family-oriented guy with two children and a devoted wife. His office was decorated with pictures of his wife and boys. He was fastidious about his appearance, was always immaculately and expensively dressed, and, at over 6 feet 5 inches tall, towered over everyone in the office.

Kim came to learn, both from her colleagues and her own observations, that Dieter had an unnerving intuition, for not just markets, but people as well. He used their foibles and weaknesses to his advantage and could be cruel. Walking past the cubicle of an overweight senior analyst, for example, he retrieved chocolate wrappers from her waste basket and, making sure that everyone else could see what he was doing, placed them in a pile on her desk.

On the other hand, when it came to looking after employees in other ways he was very generous, especially when the market was going up. Twice a year, for example, the staff enjoyed phenomenal bonus payments, parties and fabulous overseas trips—trekking through the Brazilian rainforest, whitewater-rafting down the Colorado River and visiting an ashram in the Himalayas.

Kim and Dieter worked closely for three solid months on a multimillion-dollar deal and when the deal finally closed, he invited the entire office to the Mandarin Grill to celebrate their success. When Kim arrived, rather late, she saw Dieter sitting alone sipping a martini. When she enquired where everyone else was, he simply placed a gift-wrapped Tiffany box on the table. Thinking that it was for his wife, she said nothing. It wasn't until he handed her a glass of champagne and pushed the box in her direction that she began to be alarmed. He congratulated her on the deal and told her that the box was a token of his appreciation.

She responded by gently pushing the package back towards him, saying she couldn't accept it because in bringing about a successful conclusion to the negotiations she had only been doing her job. She thanked him for his support in this but also made it very clear that she was not interested in anything more than a working relationship with him. The evening ended awkwardly.

Kim dismissed the incident as a one-off arising from the euphoria of sealing the deal. Nevertheless, she took care to avoid the possibility of similar occurrences and when Dieter asked her out for dinner or lunch, she always declined unless some of her colleagues were also going to be present. She was straightforward in all her dealings with Dieter and there were no obvious repercussions from her refusals.

As the market went through ups and downs, however, so did Dieter's moods, and the staff had learned to expect that he would take out his frustrations on them, particularly the women. It quickly became obvious, though, that the majority of his irrational behavior was directed at Kim, who was taken off projects involving the top clients, excluded from meetings and publicly berated for very minor mistakes.

The complaints among the female staff, though never expressed publicly, began to mount up—men-only golf outings,

(continued)

harbor cruises with scantily clad women, late-night pub crawls—all of which brought back memories of the testosterone-driven behavior Kim thought she'd left behind in New York. The bullying behavior increased and a few of her junior colleagues began to mutter about bringing harassment charges. Nothing much came of this, however, and they either suffered in silence or left the firm without making a formal complaint.

Staff turnover, principally among the women, was at an all-time high but Dieter simply dismissed those who left as weaklings, unable to take the heat or success. *They* were the problem and he was better off without them.

Kim stayed for as long as she could stand it but, in the end, decided that the entire industry had a perennial dose of priapism, and moved on.

Conflicts such as these can provoke two reactions: fight or flight. Leaving is sometimes the better option, yet if one chooses flight, nothing is resolved. It may make sense to leave a hostile environment, but the underlying problem doesn't go away. In the best of all possible worlds, workplaces like this would not exist; unfortunately, many still do. A better solution in such circumstances would be to seek advice and search for a positive outcome that benefits you and the organization. This takes courage in facing up to your inner fears. Many are afraid a lawsuit will sully their reputation in the marketplace, hindering chances of future employment. But seeking legal advice does not equate to a lawsuit. The reality is that not acting brings more problems. As the preacher Billy Graham once said, courage is contagious; once you act, others will too.

Whether you choose to look at these issues as sexual harassment, or as attempts to exert control and power, or as simply unbelievable, the fact remains that many women encounter similar problems in their working lives. When asked by my workshop participants how to deal with these situations, I outline the following tips on how to handle psychological or sexual harassment:

- Remain professional at all times, or a little more formal than usual, as the situation demands.
- Never think you need to entertain remarks, actions or comments or flirt with your manager to gain approval or advance your career. Be direct and specific in stating that certain behavior is unwelcome and unacceptable.
- If you're not sure about the intent of a particular comment or action directed towards you, be brutally direct in drawing attention to it, or make a joke and move on.
- When appropriate, talk about your husband/kids/fiancé/partner, and make it clear that you have no intention of reciprocating any advances.
- Being visible—showing up at events, dinners and after-hours drinks—is all part of savvy self-promotion. If you've been invited to an event and feel uncomfortable, invite a colleague—male or female—to go with you.
- Talk to your firm's ethics committee, HR department or Employee Resource or Advisor Group. They may provide access to legal advice. If not, you may wish to consult a lawyer yourself.
- US multinationals have a clear harassment policy, which includes protection for the employee but may not guarantee anonymity.

The good news is that the demographics are driving change. The management-consulting firm Booz & Company put it this way:

> As growing numbers of women enter the economic mainstream, they will have a profound effect on global business. A huge and fast-growing group of people are poised to take their place in the economic mainstream over the next decade, as producers, consumers, employees, and entrepreneurs.

This group's impact on the global economy will be at least as significant as that of China and India's billion-plus populations. But its members have not yet attracted the level of attention they deserve . . .[3]

More women are consumers, employees and entrepreneurs, and this power shift will drive change such that organizations will become more humane—which may ultimately reduce the negative power plays and sexual harassment that are the hallmark of some organizations today. As Eisler (2005) sees it, there are two forces shaping change inside organizations today—women and organizational structure—characterized by "a move away from hierarchies of domination to hierarchies of actualization based on creative power, the power to help and to nurture and with the collective power to accomplish goals together, as in teamwork. All of this is directly related to changes in gender roles and relations."

ENDNOTES

1. EEOC data: http://www.eeoc.gov/eeoc/statistics/enforcement/sexual _harassment.cfm. See also: http://www.sexualharassmentsupport.org/ SHworkplace.html
2. For full details, see Kontominas 2010.
3. http://www.booz.com/me/home/what_we_think/40007409/40007869/ 48487877

Conclusion

It has been my intention throughout this book to provide a practical, common-sense approach to building the political savvy skills necessary for leadership, for career management, for selling ideas and for navigating organizational change. As we have seen, one of the biggest hurdles to be overcome in this endeavor lies in getting people to acknowledge that politics even exists in the workplace and to embrace the notion that "politics" and "power" are not words that should engender the kind of fear and loathing that is generally exhibited by the majority who hear them spoken of in relation to the workplace.

I have found through my workshops over many years that once they are able to reframe their thinking about these words, the majority of participants begin to see their careers and the inner workings of the organizations by which they are employed in a completely different and more positive light. Many express the wish that they had only known these things earlier in their careers. The good news is that it is never too late to become more savvy in taking a more active and intentional approach towards developing and shaping your career in the direction you want.

My own thinking on organizational politics and the factors that can promote or hinder careers has been honed and shaped by the experiences shared by the participants in my workshops—of which readers have had just a taste through the various case studies outlined in the pages of this book.

Becoming savvy is not difficult to achieve, although it does require a willingness to step out of comfort zones and to confront and overcome fears and prejudices that may be so deep-seated that they are no longer recognized for what they are. While there is much to be said for individual coaching on savvy skills, there are incredible benefits to be drawn from the wisdom of groups of smart people who come together to discuss savvy and how this knowledge applies to work. Unlike other management-development workshops, savvy can be practiced immediately.

James and Arroba's work on Reading and Carrying outlined earlier is the crux of the political model of behavior. No two situations are the same, yet many managers apply the tried and tested method over and over again without reflecting on the specific situation at hand. Not many stop and think what is required in a particular situation or reflect on why someone is giving information. I am not suggesting being suspicious of coffee meetings, or encouraging paranoid thinking, but I do recommend listening, questioning and reflecting.

Understanding the nature of power and identifying where it lies within any given organization is a critical component of political savvy in the workplace. Yet there is often a general resistance or squeamishness associated with this notion. (Whenever I sense this in my conversations with workshop participants, I tend to use the phrase "soft power"—coined by Joseph Nye (see Nye 2004) and associated with collaboration, rather than inducements and threats. The phrase seems to be in vogue and is often discussed in the context of cross-cultural leadership and global expansion.)

Too often, "power" is associated with military might or command-and-control regimes, and it is not surprising, therefore, that it meets with resistance. While some employees associate power with a coercive management, this thinking needs to shift. A better way is to consider power in terms of decision making, organizational effectiveness and *how things get done*. Being connected to influential decision-makers is always helpful. In addition, embracing power and working collaboratively within these networks can help provide the much-needed work/life balance organizations are striving to achieve. While most managers find it easy to examine power when brokering business deals externally, too few feel comfortable thinking about power in relation to careers and selling ideas internally.

One manager I coached was about to lose his job because of his inability to build relationships across the organization. He had a few solid relationships but did not consider reaching out to this group for feedback or advice on projects. Instead, he preferred to work alone or closely with one internal client. He rarely discussed or shared his work before a meeting, believing that this would spoil the impact, waste time or perhaps that someone would steel his thunder. At meetings, although he distributed detailed, perfectly formatted documents, he could get very little support for his ideas, no matter how brilliant. Sadly, both the organization and that manager lost time and great ideas, but, it doesn't have to be this way. Building coalitions for support makes financial sense. Yet many managers view this as manipulative or unscrupulous. It is all a matter of reframing thinking.

As we saw with the example of Frank in Chapter 1, the focus needs to be on the meetings that take place *before* the crucial meeting; the presentation is the icing on the cake but the real dialogue takes place months in advance. Some miss this very important point, relying too much on data and rigorous calculations and not enough on the human side of decision making. A humanistic approach to decision making is critical, yet often forgotten and rarely taught in business schools. Most MBA courses reinforce the idea of mechanics and metrics and completely miscalculate how organizations work. Everyone can read charts and interpret data, but the real skill is aligning the stakeholders' thinking and beliefs. Behind-the-scenes networking and lobbying for support is critical to success.

If there is resistance, it can be addressed *before* the meeting. Attempting to deal with complex issues *during* the meeting is ludicrous and futile and will only serve to derail the conversation and delay the outcome. Lobbying behind the scenes builds coalitions and enables stakeholders to understand the project in greater detail and allows time to frame cohesive argument. At the meeting itself, everyone is not only on board but now has time for innovative thinking. Everyone wins. Leveraging the unique, human qualities inside organizations can provide a competitive advantage.

Reframing power and politics begins with middle management. Lord Acton's axiom that power tends to corrupt and absolute power corrupts absolutely needs to be eradicated from organizational mindsets. In fact, powerlessness within organizations infiltrates the minds of management and causes malaise, staff turnover, and inefficiencies. The sad reality is that organizations lose talented managers because they are either ill-equipped to navigate the unwritten rules, or fearful of embracing politics. Most organizations do not teach savvy and few managers learn the necessary skills too late. Others put their heads down and hope "it" will go away.

While organizations continue to invest in leadership and management development, not much time is spent on understanding politics and power. Courses on political savvy rarely make it on to the management curriculum of universities and business schools. Oddly enough, almost every leadership competency framework has "savvy" or some derivative of it listed. Political savvy is listed at number 48 out of 67 leadership competencies listed by Lombardo and Eichinger (2002). A skillful savvy manager, these authors say, has the "ability to navigate complex political situations effectively and quietly." Like Baddeley and James, they highlight the pitfalls of being unaware of politics and the impact this can have on careers. In my experience, every organization has a competency framework highlighting political savvy, yet most do little to support the development of this competency. Some organizations see this as a skill-building exercise that is best left to executive coaching. This is a start but it makes more sense to develop this more broadly throughout the organization.

Everyone comes to work with intelligence. Intelligence gets you to the interview and in the organizational door. But, once inside, moving from being a valued individual contributor to being a manager requires people-management skills—emotional intelligence or EQ—focusing on understanding the emotions of self, others and the team. To measure this skill, many organizations use Goleman's EQ Assessment (see Goleman 1999).

Interestingly, though political savvy is mentioned in Goleman's book, it is rarely the focus of the EQ assessment. Far too many organizations equate EQ with PQ, which can be misleading, and too few examine political savvy in their leadership-selection processes. Goleman asserts that mediocre performers lack savvy skills while outstanding performers have typically received advice and guidance on navigating organizations from a savvy mentor.

Although savvy skills may be recognized as important and, indeed, essential competencies, there is not enough emphasis on how to develop them.

As I hope this book has shown, having an understanding and connection to power is the cornerstone of savvy. When this is in place, the next step is to learn the value of self-promotion and being visible. Again, as we have seen through numerous examples in earlier chapters, this notion meets with strong resistance from people whose character or culture runs counter to the whole idea. While communication workshops are available in abundance, many employees still feel uneasy and uncomfortable with self-promotion.

But the nature of work and of organizations has changed. As organizations extend globally, matrix management expands, technology provides virtual work and virtual leadership, and many have bosses sitting thousands of miles away. In such circumstances, how can anyone know what anyone else is doing?

This new way of working will not change and will continue to evolve into different forms. Since the 2008 financial crisis, travel budgets have been slashed and layers of management removed: organizations are flat and getting flatter every year. Virtual conferencing is becoming the norm. This may be good news for innovation and decision making, but it is challenging for leadership and talent retention. Employees talk about having to do the work of three people and leaders discuss the challenges of multiple reporting lines and having too many direct reports. The bottom line is that if you do not keep people informed of what you do, no-one will know. Self-promotion is directly linked to power networks in more ways than one. Knowing this group provides a network of connections to channel communications about you and your team. The group is now working for you! It works both ways, but only if you embrace self-promotion.

If you manage people, any reticence you may have with regard to self-promotion must change quickly; the team expects this of you. I coached one executive who adamantly refused to talk about her accomplishments: self-promotion was out of the question and if this is what the company required, she would leave. One of her goals, she said, was to ensure that her team was promoted. It was only in hearing herself say these words that she began to see the difficulty of accomplishing this task without self-promotion. Though reluctant at first, she now saw the value in being recognized for her work and began by sending email broadcasts to an extensive network on the accomplishments, value, and lessons learned by both individual members of the team and the team as a whole.

We need to move away from the limiting belief that self-promotion is pretentious bragging. Granted, it can be; but this all depends on how it is done and if there is substance behind the gesture. Talking about what you do is sharing and managing knowledge. Undoubtedly, there are cultural complications with this statement. Self-promotion is easier said than done, particularly if you have been raised not to talk about what you do. But there are innovative and legitimate means to promote yourself and your team.

We spoke earlier about the value of having informal power maps as an aid to understanding social networks and for determining the power brokers within an organization. More importantly, they also show how you are connected to these groups. Uzzi and Dunlap (2005) recommend creating a list of names of the people making introductions for you. You may start to see a pattern when the same name appears on multiple lists; this person is the connector inside your network. We all know connectors: these are the people who seem to know or be connected with everyone. They can recommend an expert for any topic or project and are willing to make introductions. If you are reluctant to promote yourself, find a connector, share what you do and have them talk and connect you. Reframe your thinking and behave like a social network. You only need one connector.

There are many ways to build your profile, maintain visibility, and manage perceptions through professional networks and communities. Never underestimate the role of technology in this—from online communities to internet radio, blogs and podcasts. LinkedIn, Facebook, Twitter and Tumblr are powerful in providing avenues to share knowledge, build an expert profile and manage your brand. While you don't want to give away corporate trade secrets, these networks build not only your profile but that of your organization too. The rise of internet radio and podcasts is another inexpensive option, linking multiple platforms and countries. And finally, don't forget the power of teaching: facilitating a workshop or joining a dialogue session can go a long way to building good will and your profile. After you've conducted a workshop, send an email or write a short article on the benefits of the workshop and be sure to include the results of the evaluations. These are all simple tasks that are part of your role and benefit you, your team and the organization.

Political savvy is a critical leadership skill and one that is always in demand. Forget what you learned in school; reframe your thinking and return to the original definition of politics—*to build coalitions for the good of the organization.* For any individual who wishes to think innovatively, sell your ideas and, at the same time, move ahead in your career, working efficiently but maintaining a healthy work/ life balance, it is vital to become fully engaged in the political arena within your organization.

But it's not just individuals who need to adopt and learn these skills. Organizations, too, need to do a lot more to educate themselves and their employees on the benefits of being politically savvy. The ability to retain talented employees and develop ethical leaders is essential for the long-term health of any organization. This can be achieved by following these simple steps:

1. Make it your goal to ensure that everyone in the organization is politically savvy.
2. Create a culture where positive politics operates. Build awareness through workshops, coaching and mentoring in such things as ethical self-promotion and managing perceptions.
3. Create advocacy and mentors for all employees—particularly those outside or away from power networks—to ensure that all are connected and visible to decision makers.
4. Rewrite job descriptions with savvy vocabulary and redesign management and leadership curriculums to include the development of savvy skills.

5. Develop orientation programs and processes for new or newly promoted employees.

6. Forget performance reviews, encourage conversations!

By adopting and implementing these and other practical ideas set out in this book, individuals and organizations will, I believe, see the power of positive politics in the workplace and will reap the many benefits it has to offer.

Bibliography

Aaker, D. 1991. *Managing Brand Equity: Capitalizing on the Value of a Brand Name*. New York: The Free Press.

Adams, G. L., D. C. Treadway and L. P. Stepina 2008. "The role of disposition in politics perception formation: The predictive capacity of negative and positive affectivity, equity sensitivty, and self-efficacy." *Journal of Managerial Issues*, Winter.

Aguirre, D., and K. Sabbagh 2010. The Third Billion. *Strategy + Business*. Booz & Company, Summer Issue 59.

Babcock, L., and D. Laschever 2003. *Women Don't Ask: Negotiation and the Gender Divide*. New Jersey: Princeton University Press.

Baddeley, S., and K. James 1987. "Owl, Fox, Donkey or Sheep: Political Skills for Managers," *Management Learning*: 18(3).

Baddeley, S., and K. James 1991. "The Power of Innocence: From Politeness to Politics." *Management Education and Development* 22(2).

Blakeley, L. 2008, "What is a Results Only Work Environment?" at: http://www.bnet.com/article/what-is-a-results-only-work-environment/ 237128 (September 25).

Bohman, L., and T. Deal 2008. *Reframing Organization, Artistry, Choice and Leadership*. 4th Edition. San Francisco: Jossey-Bass.

Brandon, R., and M. Seldman 2004. *Survival of the Savvy: High-Integrity Political Tactics for Career and Company Success*. New York: Free Press.

Bridges, W. 2009. *Managing Transitions: Making the Most of Change*. 3rd edition. Da Capo Press.

Brogan, C. 2010a. www.chrisbrogan.com

Brogan, C. 2010b. http://myescapevelocity.com

Brogan, C., and J. Smith 2009. *Trust Agents*. New Jersey: John Wiley & Sons.

Brown, K. A., R. Ettison, and N. L. Hyer 2011. "Why Every Project Needs a Brand and How to Create One." MIT Sloan, Summer.

Buchanan, D. A. 2008. "You Stab My Back, I'll Stab Yours: Management Experience and Perceptions of Organization Political Behaviour," *British Journal of Management* 19(1).

Buchanan, D. A., and R. J. Badham 2008. *Power, Politics, and Organizational Change: Winning the Turf Game*, 2nd edition, London: Sage Publications.

Buchanan, D. A. 2008. "Interview: Power, Politics, and Organizational Change," Knowledge Interchange Podcast. Learning Services Team, Cranfield School of Management.

Carey, B. 2010. "Narcissism: The Malady of Me," *New York Times*, December 4, at: http://www.nytimes.com/2010/12/05/weekinreview/05carey.html

Carli, L. 2006. "Gender Issues in Workplace Groups: Effects of Gender and Communication Style on Social Influence" in Barrett M., and M. Davidson, *Gender and Communication at Work (Gender and Organizational Theory)*. Burlington: Ashgate Publishing Company.

Chapman, P. 2010. "Lessons of a Banking Collapse" *Financial Times*, September 14.

Cialdini, R. 2007. *Influence: The Psychology of Persuasion*. New York: Collins.

Cooper, M. 2010. "For Women Body Language Matters" at: http://www.stanford.edu/group/gender/cgi-bin/wordpressblog/2010/11/for-women-leaders-body-language-matters/

Culbert, S. 2008. "Get Rid of Performance Reviews, It destroys moral, kills teamwork, and hurts the bottom line and that's just for starters." *Wall Street Journal* at: http://online.wsj.com/article/SB122426318874844933.html

Culbert, S., and L. Rout 2010. *Get Rid of Performance Reviews! How Companies Can Stop Intimidating and Start Managing and Focus on What Really Matters*. New York: Business Plus.

Dubrin, A. 1990. *Winning Office Politics*. New Jersey: Prentice Hall.

Earley, C., S. Ang and J. Tan 2006. *CQ Developing Cultural Intelligence at Work*. Stanford: Stanford University Press.

Eisler, R. 2005. "The Economics of Enlightened Use of Power" In L. Coughlin, E. Wingard & K. Hollihan (Eds), *Enlightened Power: How Women are Transforming The Practice of Leadership*. San Francisco: Jossey-Bass.

Fischer, P. 2007. *The New Boss: How to Survive the First 100 Days*. London: Kogan Page.

Fisher-Yoshida, B., and K. Geller 2009. *Transnational Leadership Development: Preparing the Next Generation for the Borderless Business World*. New York: American Management Association.

Fishman, S. 2008. "Burning Down the House: Is Lehman's Dick Fuld the true villain in the collapse of Wall Street or is he being sacrificed for the sins of his peers?" *New York Magazine*, November 30.

Galpin, T. J., and M. Herndon 2007. *The Complete Guide to Mergers & Acquisitions: Process tools to support M&A integration at every level*. San Francisco: Jossey-Bass.

Gladwell, M. 2000. *Tipping Point: How Little Things Can Make a Big Difference*. New York: Little, Brown and Company.

Goleman, D. 1999. *Working With Emotional Intelligence*. London: Bloomsbury.

Greene, R. 2000. *The 48 Laws of Power*. London: Profile Books.

Gruenfeld, D. 2010. "Body Language Matters" at: http://www.stanford .edu/group/gender/cgi-bin/wordpressblog/2010/11/for-women-leaders-body-language-matters/

Hall, E. 1989. *Beyond Culture*. New York: Doubleday.

Handy, C. 1993. *Understanding Organizations; How Understanding the Ways Organizations Actually Work Can Be Used to Manage Them Better*. Oxford: Oxford University Press.

Hay Group 1999. Emotional Competence Inventory (ECI) Feedback Report. Hay/McBer, Diagnostics Resource Group. London: Boyatzis, Goleman & Hay Acquisition Co. Inc.

Hernez-Broome, G., C. McLaughlin and S. Trovas 2006. *Selling Yourself Without Selling Out: A Leader's Guide to Ethical Self-Promotion*. Corporate Leadership Council.

———2009. *The Truth about Sucking Up: How Authentic Self-Promotion Benefits You and the Organization*. Corporate Leadership Council.

Hiatt, J., and T. Creasey 2003. *Change Management*. Prosci Learning Center.

Hochwater, W. A., J. Matrecia, D. Johnson, and G. Ferris 2004. "The interactive effects of politics perceptions and trait cynicism on work outcomes." *Journal of Leadership and Organizational Studies*, Spring, at: http://findarticles.com/p/articles/mi_m0NXD/is_4_10/ai_n25096108/

Jagger, S. 2010. "Slap in the Face for Fuld who led Lehman Bros to its doom." *The Sunday Times*, March 13.

James, K., and T. Arroba 2005. "Reading and Carrying: A Framework for Learning about Emotion and Emotionality," *Management Learning* 36(3).

Jarrett, M. 2009. *Changeability: Why some companies are ready for change and others aren't.* FT Prentice Hall.

Jellison, J. 2006. *Managing the Dynamics of Change: The fastest Path to creating an engaged and productive workforce.* New York: McGraw Hill.

Kacmar, M., D. Bozeman, D. Carlson and W. Anthony 1999. "An Examination of the Perceptions of Organizational Politics Model: Replication and Extension," *Human Relations* 52(3).

Kanter, R. M. 2010. "Powerlessness Corrupts," *Harvard Business Review*, July–August.

Kaplan, R. 2002. *Warrior Politics: Why Leadership Demands a Pagan Ethos.* New York: Random House.

Karppinen, V. 2007. "The Role of Organizational Politics in Performance Appraisal Process," Helsinki University of Technology, BIT Research Centre, Laboratory of Work Psychology and Leadership: virpi .karppinen@tkk.fi

Kellaway, L. 2010. "It's Time to Sack Job Appraisals", *Financial Times*, July 11, at: http://www.ft.com/intl/cms/s/0/a72a8ca6-8b8e-11df-ab4d-00144feab49a.html#axzz1VTobL5mZ

Keltner, D. 2007–08. "The Paradox of Power," at: http://greatergood .berkeley.edu/article/item/power_paradox/

Kleiner, A. 2002. "Core Group Therapy," *strategy+business* 27.

———2003a. *Who Really Matters: Core Group Theory.* London: Nicholas Brealey Publishing.

———2003b. "Are you in with the in crowd?" *Harvard Business Review*, July.

———2003c. "Build your Organizational Equity," *strategy+business* 31.

Kontominas, B. 2010. "David Jones sex harassment case: publicist sues for $37m," August 2, at: http://www.smh.com.au/business/david-jones-sex-harassment-case-publicist-sues-for-37m-20100802–112iw.html

Kotter, J., and H. Rathgeber, 2005. *Our Iceberg is Melting: Changing and Succeeding Under Any Conditions.* New York: St. Martin's Press.

Kotter, J. 1996. *Leading Change.* Boston: Harvard Business School Press.

Kouzes, J., and B. Posner 2002. *Leadership Challenge.* San Francisco: Jossey-Bass.

Lehrer, J. 2010. "The Power Trip: Contrary to the Machiavellian cliché, nice people are more likely to rise to power. Then something strange happens: Authority atrophies the very talents that got them there," at: http://online.wsj.com/article/SB10001424052748704407804575425561952689390.html

Liptak, A., and S. Greenhouse 2010. "Supreme Court Agrees to Hear Wal-Mart Appeal," *New York Times*, December 6, at: http://www.nytimes.com/2010/12/07/business/07bizcourt.html

Liu, Y., J. Liu and L. Wu 2010. "Are you willing and able? Roles of motivation, power, politics in career growth," *Journal of Management* 36(3).

Livermore, D. 2010. *Leading with Cultural Intelligence.* New York: AMACOM.

Lombardo, M., and R. Eichinger 1989. *Preventing Derailment: What to do before it's too late.* Center for Creative Leadership.

——— 2002. *The Leadership Architect Suite.* Available at: www.lominger.com

London School of Economics 2009. "When performance-related pay backfires," June 24, at: http://www.finchannel.com/index.php?option=com_content&task=view&id=40997&Itemid=47

Longenecker, C., H. Sims, and D. Goia 1987. "Behind the Mask: The Politics of Employee Appraisal," *The Academy of Management Executive* (1987–89) 1(3).

Maccoby, M. 2000. "Narcissistic Leaders: The Incredible Pros and the Incredible Cons," *Harvard Business Review*, January.

Manzoni, J-F., and J-L. Barsoux 2002. *The Set-Up-to-Fail Syndrome: How Good Managers Cause Great People to Fail.* Boston: Harvard Business Press.

Maslan, J., D. Fedor, S. Farmer, and K. Bettenhausen 2005. "Perceptions of Positive and Negative Organizational Politics: Role of the Frequency and Distance of Political Behavior;" paper presented at the 2005 annual meeting of the Southern Management Association, Charlotte, South Carolina, USA.

Maurer, R. 1996. *Beyond the Wall of Resistance: Unconventional Strategies that Build Support for Change.* Austin: Bard Books.

Maurer, R. 2009. *Change without Migraines.* Maurer & Associates.

Montoya, P., and T. Vandehey 2009. *The Brand Called You: Create a Personal Brand That Wins Attention and Grows Your Business.* London: McGraw Hill.

Morgan, G. 1997. *Images of Organizations.* London: Sage.

Namie, G. 2009. "Role of Incompetence of Aggressive Bully Bosses Confirmed," at: http://www.workplacebullying.org/2009/10/14/ fast-chen/

Nardi, B., S. Whittaker, and H. Schwarz 2000. "It's not what you know, it's who you know: work in the information age," *First Monday* 5(5) at: http://firstmonday.org/issues/issue5_5/nardi/index.html

Nye, J. 2004. *Soft Power: The Means to Success in World Politics.* Massachusetts: Peruses.

Peters, T. 1997. *The Brand Called You.* Fast Company.

Pfeffer, J. 1992. *Managing with Power.* Boston: Harvard Business School Press.

———2010a. *Power; Why some people have it and others don't.* New York: Harper Collins Publishers.

———2010b. "The Narcissistic World of the MBA Student," *Financial Times*, November 7.

Phukanchana, T. 2004. "Politeness in Thai Culture: Strategies of Disagreeing;" paper presented at the annual meeting of the International Communication Association, New Orleans Sheraton, New Orleans, LA, May 27, at: http://www.allacademic.com/meta/p113365_index.html

Pink, D. 2010a. Discussions on Results Only Work Environment (ROWE) at: www.danpink.com.

———2010b. "The Surprising Science of Motivation, Ted Talks" at: http://www.ted.com/talks/dan_pink_on_motivation.html

Roffer, R. "Personal Branding Strategies" at: http://www.bigfishmarketing.com

Rooke, D., and W. Torbet 2005. "Seven Transformations of Leadership," *Harvard Business Review*, April.

Russell, J. 2001. "Are You Managing Perception? Leadership & Management Engineering," at: http://www.engr.wisc.edu/cee/faculty/russell_jeffrey/036.pdf

Shambaugh, R. (2008). *It's not a glass ceiling, It's A Sticky Floor: Free yourself from the Hidden Behaviors Sabotaging Your Career Success.* New York: McGraw Hill.

Simmons, A. 2001. *The Story Factor; Inspiration, Influence and Persuasion Through the Art of Storytelling.* Cambridge: Perseus Publishing.

Stybel, L., and M. Peabody 2005. "Friend, Foe, Ally, Adversary . . . or something else?" *MIT Sloan Management Review* 46: 4.

Sutton, R. 2007. *The No A-Hole Rule: Building A Civilized Workplace and Surviving One That Isn't.* New York: Warner.

Sutton, R. 2010. *Good Boss, Bad Boss: How to be the Best and Learn from the Worst.* New York: Hachette.

Tannen, D. 1990. *You Just Don't Understand: Men and Women in Conversation.* New York: Ballantine Books.

Tobak, S. 2010. "10 reasons why your network is your biggest asset" at: http://www.bnet.com/blog/ceo/10-reasons-why-your-network-is-your-biggest-asset/5723?tag=content;drawer-container, October 6.

Trompenaars, F. 1993. *Riding the Waves of Culture: Understanding Cultural Diversity in Business.* London: Nicholas Brealey Publishing.

Tuck, E., and T. Earl 1996 "Why CEOs Succeed and Why They Fail: Hunters and Gatherers in Corporate Life," *Strategy – Management – Competition*, October 1, at: http://www.strategy-business.com/article/12502?gko=0c23a

Uzzi, B., and S. Dunlap 2005. "How to build your network," *Harvard Business Review*, December.

Vedantam, S. 2007. "Salary and the High Cost of Negotiating," *Washington Post*, July 30, at: http://www.washingtonpost.com/wp-dyn/content/article/2007/07/29/AR2007072900827.html

Vigoda-Gadot, E. 2003. *Developments in Organizational Politics: How Political Dynamics Affect Employee Performance in Modern Work Sites.* Cheltenham: Edward Elgar Publishing.

Watkins, M. 2003. *The First 90 Days: Critical Success Strategies for New Leaders at All Levels.* Boston: Harvard Business School Press.

Wilson, J. S., and I. Blumenthal 2008. *Managing Brand You.* New York: AMACOM books.

Wu, S. 2010. "An Exploration Study of Intercultural Communication Problems of Huawei Amsterdam Branch Office," Wageningen University-Department of Social Sciences MSc Thesis Communication and Innovation Studies Group.

Zanor, C. 2010. "A Fate That Narcissists Will Hate: Being Ignored," *New York Times*, November 29, at: http://www.nytimes.com/2010/11/30/health/views/30mind.html

Index

Hinder careers, 148
Hong Kong, xi, 16, 29, 36, 53, 58, 60, 65,
   66, 107, 118, 119, 142
Hu, Jin Tao, 1
Human resources (HR), xvi, 35, 36, 53, 83,
   101, 136, 141
   Human resources department, 40, 43,
      122, 130, 136, 145
Humor, 12, 55, 98
   jokes, 28–29, 68, 89, 90, 136
   pay attention, 89, 117
   use humor, 95

I
IBM, 88
Ideas
   influencing others, decision makers, 149
   selling, unable to sell, 79, 122, 147
   stakeholder management, 4
Impact of predecessors, 61
In-depth plan, 57
India, 25, 100
Influence
   lobbying, unofffical behind the scenes, 5
   political behavior map, x, 124
Influencers, 15
Informal power, 77, 79, 153
Integrity, xv, 6, 14, 18, 19
Intel, 97
Intuitive, xvi, 2, 77

J
Japan, 25, 119
Jest, 88
Job descriptions, 57, 58, 132, 154
   rarely spell out real measurements, 80
Jockeying for position, 46
Jokes, 88, 89, 136

K
Kellaway, Lucy, 123
Kohlberg, Kravis, Roberts (KKR), 6

L
Labels, or labeled, 114, 120
Large scale change, 41, 47
Laughs, 89

Law of the few, 80, 81
Lawsuits, 125, 137, 144
Lay, Kenneth, 8
Leadership
   competency frameworks, 150–151
   criticized predecessor, 60
   cross-cultural leadership, 118
   leadership transitions, 59, 69
   politics with, 2, 8, 154
   previous incumbent, 61
Leadership presence, 92, 120
Learning, 7
Lehman Brothers, 7
Listening, xvii, 58, 81, 116, 148
LinkedIn, 77, 80, 87, 105, 153
Lobbying, 3, 5, 6, 42, 69, 150
Lockheed Martin, 125

M
Malaysia, 71, 126
Management
   executive management, 27, 87–88
   feedback from management, 74,
      122, 129
   middle management, 17, 22, 150
   senior management, 28, 37, 81
Mandarin, 27, 109, 128
Marketing, 103
MBA programs
   courses, 150
Meetings
   power in the room, 12, 49
Mentors
   sponsors or advocates, 88
Mergers and acquisitions (M&A), 41, 47
Merkel, Angela, 1
Mintzberg, Henry, 2
Misinterpret, 114
Mr. or Ms. Nice, 64
Myers-Briggs
   introversion, extroversion, 73
   preferences for, 32

N
Naive, xvii, 16, 23, 41, 42
Narcissism, 69
Navigating organizations, 147, 151